Raising

WILL

Raising WILL
Surviving the Brilliance and Blues of ADHD

Katherine Quie, PhD, LP

wise ink | minneapolis

RAISING WILL © copyright 2019 by Katherine Quie.

ISBN 13: 978-1-63489-217-9

Library of Congress Catalog Number: 2019935460
Printed in the United States of America
First Printing: 2019
23   22   21 20 19   5   4   3   2   1

Cover and interior design by Mary Austin Speaker

807 Broadway St. NE, Suite 46
Minneapolis, MN 55413
wiseink.com

For my father—you will always be in my heart.

And for William—thank you for encouraging me to share our story.

CONTENTS

ACKNOWLEDGMENTS

I would like to acknowledge the children and families who have taught me so much about ADHD over the last twenty years. Without you, this book would not have been written.

I am forever grateful to my husband, Bill, for supporting my writing life, especially since he would prefer chucking our belongings and living in a tent in the mountains.

Thank you, Emma, for your calm, wise soul, and for not guilting me when I left the house to write.

I want to thank the rest of my relatives (this includes you, Mom), who love me no matter what.

I owe much thanks to Cheri Register and Elizabeth Jarrett Andrew, my writing teachers from the former Foreword Program at the Loft Literary Center. You were always honest, yet supportive, which kept me going. And thanks to Amy Hallberg, a graduate of Foreword, Wise Ink author, and the best writing partner ever.

To my YMCA Ladies, long-time besties, Healing Elements yogis, Psych Recovery colleagues, and those who fill me up—you are all so appreciated.

AUTHOR'S NOTE

In the very beginning, this book was my journal. I wrote daily. As the years drew on and I realized I was writing a "book," I had to rely on memory to recreate parts of our story to fulfill the narrative arc. I also changed the names and identifying characteristics of nearly all professionals to maintain their privacy. That being said, this is a true story.

Prologue

I decided to write this book over a decade ago. I was new to Saint Paul, and I needed an outlet. My husband, Bill, listened as well as any good Lutheran, but I needed more than he could offer. Way more. I could have picked up the phone and called a close friend, but then I'd have to ask about her life, and sometimes, especially when the kids were little, I didn't have the strength.

This book became my Minnesota bestie. It let me pour my feelings onto the page without strings attached. It let me be selfish—indulgent, even. Bill called me out on it a few times: "How long could you *possibly* work on the same book? You don't need fancy writing classes. You're already a good writer."

Nothing could speed up my process. My book would take as long as I needed it to take. It helped me figure stuff out, like how to balance a career while parenting two high-needs kids.

In the beginning, writing was all release. Who cared what I typed? I was the only one reading it. I wrote about my loneliness in the Midwest and minor grievances, like being invited to parties and being left to stare at people's backs while they gathered in tight circles (something southern hosts simply cannot do—even if they hate the person's guts, bless their souls). I wrote about my chronic self-doubt, my bitterness toward stay-at-home moms, my bitterness toward my toddler daughter's double personality (super compliant in public, brittle at home), and my son William's budding ADHD—except I didn't call it ADHD back then. I also wrote about all of the terrible people who got just as annoyed with him as I did.

A few years later, at a party, I whispered to my friend Missy about my "writing."

"What are you writing about?" she whispered back.

"Oh, I'm not really writing." I cringed. "I'm just, you know . . . umm, jotting my thoughts down."

She wondered if I'd heard of the Loft, a writing center in Minneapolis. I hadn't. She thought I should check it out.

Everything felt different after that discussion. What *was* I doing anyway? I stared at my one-hundred-page rant with disappointment. It was a big fat journal entry. But I didn't want to stop. I needed the friendship, the support.

That's when I realized that deep, deep down, beneath my insecurities, I wanted to write a book about our life. I just didn't know how.

So I enrolled in a writing class at the Loft. My first creative-writing teacher—a Scandinavian woman from

Albert Lee, Minnesota—wrote honest prose about her working-class roots. She assigned readings from authors like James Baldwin, Anne Lamott, Maya Angelou, and Stephen King. I learned about inner and outer story, characterization, and how to write hooks between chapters.

In college, I'd focused on the sciences. I'd followed the same path in graduate school to become a child psychologist. Creative writing was so different, so freeing and soulful, especially compared to the technical writing involved in my profession.

Shortly afterward, I applied for a two-year creative writing apprenticeship at the Loft. I finished with a rough, incomplete manuscript, largely about raising William. A few years after that, I hired an editor who had won a book award. Then I hired another.

Somewhere along the way, my reasons for writing changed. At work, when parents fretted over their kids with ADHD, I understood. When I shared my experiences, parents took off their glasses, leaned in close, and questioned: "What helped? What was a waste of time? Did your son take medicine? Get special ed? Tutors? *How* did you get him to do his homework?"

In the end, I wrote this book to share an honest perspective about how ADHD can impact a family. I felt an obligation to clear up some misconceptions, too. ADHD is way more than a DSM-5 diagnosis that causes inattention and hyperactivity. It's pervasive, meaning it impacts many aspects of development. I wanted people to see ADHD for what it is: a strength *and* a pain in the butt.

Since I've had the opportunity to evaluate hundreds of kids with ADHD as part of my profession, I've woven in bits and pieces of what I've learned in this capacity too.

ADHD can turn the kindest parents into harsh Nervous Nellies who say things like: "Mark, you'd better have the house key soldered to your shoe. Don't you *dare* put us in danger by losing another goddamned key!"

ADHD can cause those who have it to become big fat liars too: "Don't worry about a thing, Mom. I turned in that paper yesterday. The teacher doesn't keep up with her gradebook." After a lifetime of disappointing loved ones, lying is often a hell of a lot easier for a child than saying something like, "Mom, I really can't remember anything except facts about my video games."

But ADHD doesn't always change us for the worst. It can make us way more patient too. And patience is imperative if you love someone with ADHD. Otherwise, you'll chip away at their soul . . . and yours.

PART ONE:
Early Days

Blues Kids

"Mommy, when does William play?" Emma asked as she scooped another bite of her massive chocolate sundae.

I scanned the Hard Rock Cafe for William's blond hair and the other preteens in his group, but I couldn't see through the thick crowd. I was dying of thirst and relieved to be in air-conditioning, given the ninety-degree Chicago heat. Bill had gone to the bar to get us a beer.

"Who knows," I said with an apologetic shrug. A week earlier, we had driven from our home, Saint Paul, to Chicago so that William could attend Blues Camp, a nonprofit organization with a mission to promote blues among youth. We had heard about the camp one evening after William performed at Famous Dave's Blues Club in Minneapolis. It was a Tuesday, open mic night, the only evening amateurs could perform with a real blues band.

Thankfully, Emma, now nine, loved bar food. She had been to a handful of bars by now, something I could never have predicted. During her adoption process, the Chinese government required Bill and me to sign documents professing our strong moral character. We promised to give our daughter an excellent education and rich family experiences. I knew the Chinese wouldn't have considered bringing Emma to blues bars a rich family experience, but we couldn't get too stuck on details. We were doing our best.

Bill joined us at the table a few minutes later with two well-needed pints of beer.

"I just saw William. His group plays last," he said with a frown. We both knew what that meant. There were at least five groups of blues kids slotted to perform. It had been a long week, and we had a six-hour drive ahead of us. That's when William's group instructor, Franki, approached our table.

"Your boy's a natural front man," he said with a wide, joyous smile, sinking his hands deep into his pockets.

"Thanks," I said, semi-surprised he knew who we were. Hundreds of kids attended camp each summer. I had no idea what a front man was, but it sounded good.

"William's got the high energy and talent of a front man in a band; he's our lead singer and guitarist this week," he said, tapping his fingers on the table.

Then he disappeared into the crowd.

Franki's words lifted me up. The night before, I'd looked him up on the internet, curious about his background. Images of Franki's smiling face filled my computer screen. He had turned professional at fifteen and played with blues greats like Ray Charles, Curtis Mayfield, and Bill Withers. I knew that William had a knack for music, but hearing it from a seasoned musician gave me hope that he would land on his feet.

I Think I Can

Unlike other toddlers, who cried the first twenty minutes of flights and crashed in their parent's arms, William remained as alert as an army officer on night watch. His blue eyes scanned his surroundings and then landed back on me, his main source of entertainment.

I stared back at him, searching for the normal signs of fatigue: a drooping eyelid, bobbing head, or long stretch of quiet.

Please, God, I thought. Make him stop talking, stop moving.

One flight, William sat wide-eyed next to me in his throne. "Mommy, read it again," he said, holding up *The Little Engine That Could*, whacking me in the forehead with the spine.

"Okay, one more time. Then it's time to close your eyes and rest."

William crawled into my lap and swept his fingers through my long blonde hair as I read the book one last time. When I tilted him back in my lap for a snooze, he squirmed out of my hands, onto the floor, and into the aisle.

"Get back here, buddy," I said, unbuckling, booking after him.

"No, Mommy! I'm running!" he yelled, arching his back.

When he tried to break free again, I brought out plan B: Tupperware of all sizes packed with treats. As he flung Cheerios and raisins into the aisle, I tried to avoid eye contact with the passengers. Why did I fly solo across the country with an eighteen-month-old?

"Read to me, Mommy," William said, slipping the book into my hands.

I-think-I-can, I-think-I-can, I repeated in my head.

William was my little engine that could.

The question was, could I?

✳

The next time I flew with William, Bill and I had a better plan.

"Here's some yogurt, buddy," I said, blocking him from running yet another circle around the gate area.

William opened wide, took a bite, and paused mid-chew. "It's not my yogurt," he said, eyes watering.

"Really? It's your favorite, Yoplait vanilla custard." Bill and I glanced at each other, holding back grins. The pediatrician had recommended half a capsule of Benadryl for the flight.

My in-laws paid for the whole family to fly to Ireland for their fiftieth wedding anniversary. We were jazzed about sightseeing, meeting quirky locals, savoring fish and chips, and of course, the party. But we cringed at the thought of bringing our two-year-old.

Fifteen minutes later, as we waited in line to board the plane, William sat down hard at our feet.

I raised my eyebrows at Bill. "I can't believe this."

"Believe what?"

"That he isn't running. That we drugged our baby. Who does that?" I whispered.

"We do," Bill answered with a smirk, scooping William up in his arms.

That's why I married you, I thought. You don't second-guess. It was a red-eye. Now we could sleep all the way to Dublin. We'd brought our own blankets and tiny pillows. I couldn't wait to relax.

*

"Mommy!" William screamed, pinching the crap out of my arm within minutes of takeoff.

"What? What's the matter, buddy?" I asked, rubbing his back.

"Let me go!"

Bill and I looked at each other in confusion.

"I NEEED TO GET DOWWWN!" he screamed, thrashing like a bucking bronco.

Bill reached to pull William into his lap, but he lost his grip.

My hands shook as I tried to unbuckle myself and chase after him.

"STOP!"

"What's the matter? Are you hurt?" I asked, holding him, forcing eye contact, searching for the boy I knew.

"I want DOWN!"

My only choice was to walk him up and down the aisle. Some passengers pretended to read; others whispered to their spouses and shook their heads in disapproval.

Some offered suggestions: Milk to clear his ears? Nilla wafers to settle his stomach? Gingerroot? One mother waved a bottle of Children's Tylenol overhead.

"NO THANKS, WE TRIED IT," I yelled over William's screams. Bill and I had squirted the purple goo into his mouth, but he spit it out like poison.

Two hours into our eleven-hour flight, a platinum-blonde flight attendant approached me near the bathrooms. "You *have* to do something," she said.

"What?" I asked, pushing William's gaping mouth away from my ear. Rings of sweat had formed under my arms. Couldn't she see I was in the middle of a marathon wrestling match?

"Your *child*. You have to do something about his crying."

"Here, you take him," I said, shoving him at her.

She thrust her arms forward, wide-eyed.

"AHHH," William screeched, grasping for me.

This behavior continued over most of the Atlantic.

✳

The next morning, I scanned my surroundings. Bill, his sister Katie, our teenage nieces Jana and Krista, and our five-year-old nephew Luke were asleep in their seats. William lay on his side with his legs curled up in the rebirth yoga position. He had fallen asleep on the floor of the plane by my feet around sunrise. Red cheeks and puffy eyes were the only remnants of his monstrosity. I had a few too: scratched arms and a pounding headache.

Draw a Snowman

Our plan was to caravan from Dublin to Killarney, a quaint town known for its national park, castles, and medieval forts. My in-laws had rented villas for the family there. Who knows why Jana agreed to join us in our car. Maybe she thought William's sleeplessness on the flight was a one-time thing. She'd only met him a few times.

I admired Jana's pluck. She was quick to smile and wise for a teen. She'd helped raise her younger brother, Luke. She cooled his soup and encouraged him to climb up one more rung on the jungle gym.

"Jana, draw a snowman," William instructed a few minutes into our drive.

"Sure, William. What color snowman do you want?"

"A red one."

"Okay, here's a red one," she answered sketching a few strokes on the paper.

"Now draw a hat and buttons," he added, thrusting the notepad back.

"Sure."

"Now draw a baby green one."

"Okay."

"Now make a snowman family."

I visualized each circular stroke. I'd drawn over a hundred the last few weeks. Snowmen were William's latest obsession. Before that, it was Buzz Lightyear. Before that, the Teletubbies.

"Does William ever sleep in the car?" Jana asked forty-five minutes into our drive.

Bill and I glanced at each other and smiled. "Not much," I answered.

I'd rarely witnessed William burn someone else out, and the fact that he was tiring a seasoned teenager felt validating. He'd only been with Anoop, his day care provider, and us. We rarely hired babysitters. Bill's salary in private practice as a defense attorney was unpredictable. I had no income as a graduate student. Cost of living was high in Seattle.

Anoop had known William since he was eight weeks old. When I dropped him off at her home on my school days, she'd smiled at him and knelt down open-armed in one of her colorful saris.

"Will-iam," she'd say in her thick Eastern Indian accent. "Let's go read Buzz Lightyear. He's still your favorite, yes?"

William released me and toddled toward her without looking back.

If I complained to Anoop about his nonstop movement or lack of sleep, she'd pause, a knowing look on her face.

"Katherine, I think I knew him in past life," she'd said. "He has much to do in this life. He's a special boy. My husband says this too."

He's special all right, I thought, appreciating her kindness.

※

That evening, the whole family met at a pub in Killarney. The musty gray cobblestone building, built in the 1600s, resembled a mini prison. On the inside, round mahogany tables and sturdy chairs brought the place to life. Large colored-glass, Tiffany-style fixtures hung from the ceiling over each crowded table, giving off a warm hue.

I pulled my chair up beside Bill and his family. Luke colored in his seat, flanked by his older sisters. I bounced William on my knees to distract him from his ultimate desire: freedom to roam. The bar was loud and packed with people.

Please don't let him go into freak-out mode like he did on the plane, I prayed. A waiter tucked a wooden high chair at the table beside me. "Thank you," I said, catching the man's eyes before he whisked off.

"Look, buddy, the nice man brought you a seat,"

I said, hoisting William into the chair. I brushed my hands up and down the legs and back of the chair. Then I got down on my hands and knees and visibly inspected it.

My heart sank.

"There's no seat belt," I told Bill.

"He'll be fine. Stop worrying," he said, squeezing my hand. "Check out the beers on tap. What do you want?"

My instinct was to pout. Or cry. My husband was a rat. It was 2001, not 1950. Who the hell did he think he was, enjoying himself with his family while I was drowning with our son? Situations like this triggered my pent-up resentment about the injustices between men and women.

But I couldn't crack.

I was surrounded by Lutherans.

When things got tense, they packed up their emotions into a tight ball and swallowed them. They focused on the good things. They didn't complain. My father-in-law, Dr. Paul Quie, grew up farming in Northfield. He described Yale Medical School as a breeze compared to farming. My mother-in-law, Ms. Betty Quie, a Wellesley graduate, raised four kids nearly solo given Paul's all-consuming career. She rarely lost her cool. It just wasn't in her blood.

My parents were the opposite. As a Texan litigator, my dad literally fought for a living. Young lawyers lined up to watch him tangle people up in their own words in court. My mother was a Unitarian artist who bucked authority. I was mild-mannered compared to my parents but fiery compared to the Quies.

As I scanned the beers on tap, William stood up in the high chair and teetered forward.

"Sit down," I said, holding him by the waist.

"Mommy, look!" William said, pointing to the bag-pipe players.

I nudged Bill. "Will you take William?"

Bill reached out his arms with a smile. "Come here, buddy."

"NOOO! MOMMY!" William yelled, burying his head in my chest.

Bill and I exchanged a look. His eyes said, I will rip William from your arms if you want me to, but it could get ugly.

I couldn't do it, not after the plane ride.

William and I waded through the crowd to check out the Celtic band, his warm cheek against mine. A harpist lightly plucked a simple melody in the background along with bagpipes and a quick fiddle. I stood on my tiptoes to peer at the band over the crowd. The men wore pleated red plaid kilts, blazers, and black tweed caps. The harp-ist wore a traditional Celtic dress with a tight bodice and a long, flowing red plaid skirt.

I'd grown up hearing tales of my father's Irish Catholic relatives, the Sheehans and Horrigans. I had been Katherine Horrigan for twenty-three years before I became a Quie. I wondered if my ancestors had ventured here years ago.

"Let's go, Mommy!" William yelled, pointing to the musicians, his eyes wide. "I want to be with them."

"That's their stage, buddy. We have to stand back here."

"I want to be up there with them," he said, pointing to center stage.

For the next half hour, William remained still in my arms, transfixed by the music. I was thankful for his calm body, but I didn't think much of it beyond that.

When the band took a break, William and I returned to the table. Bill reached over to pat my leg, a pint of Guinness in hand. I made out bits and pieces of the family conversation; someone made a birdie on a par four, someone duffed the final hole and landed in a sand trap.

I sank into my seat and closed my eyes. This was not what I'd expected for our first big vacation. I'd fantasized about Bill's parents and siblings taking William off my hands.

"Mommy, they're playing again," William said, pushing my eyelids open, pointing to the stage.

"William, sit down," I said, slipping his legs out from under him.

"Let's go, Mommy!"

This time, I pushed him down hard like the strung-out mothers I'd judged at Target. The look of surprise on his face jolted me out of my anger.

"WE'RE GOING FOR A WALK!" I yelled in Bill's ear. I slung William on my hip and wove through the crowd.

I walked out of the pub and set William down. We

walked hand-in-hand at a clipped pace. He toddled beside me in his navy Keds, the only shoes that he could tolerate.

William and I passed a neighborhood grocery, a tiny bookstore, and pubs on each corner, dark green with red doors. The cobblestone streets gave me comfort. They'd been there for hundreds of years, holding people up. I envisioned horses pulling carriages of Irish folks into town, men in their top hats and overcoats, women in their embroidered velvet dresses with fur wraps.

We passed scruffy, kind-faced men in thick, cream-colored sweaters. They sipped beer with their friends on street corners and tipped their hats at me and my wide-eyed boy. William didn't seem to notice. He was drawn to bigger things.

"What's that, Mommy?" he asked, pointing at a musty, ancient church and then even higher to the slender steeple at the tip-top. I crouched beside him and followed his tiny finger.

"That's the steeple of the church," I answered, tucking a wisp of hair behind his ear.

"What's a steeple for?"

"Maybe it's to help people find their way to church, to God," I answered, shrugging my shoulders.

"Who's God?" William asked, leaning into me, rubbing my hair.

My brain froze. He might as well have asked me to describe hybridization in organic chemistry. I'd never even read the Bible. But if there were a God, now would be a really good time for her to show up.

＊

Here He Comes

From childbirth forward, nothing had gone as expected. At the hospital, the first nurse accidentally broke my water with her pointy, fuchsia fake nails. The next reassured me that if I wanted an epidural, all I had to do was ask. Two hours later, my pain was so great that I had dug half-moon gashes into my palms. Later, Bill confided that the ghostly look on my face and series of mishaps at the hospital made him fear the worst. Finally, he'd stormed down to the nurses' station.

"Where the hell is the doctor? My wife was told she could get an epidural any time. This has gone on for hours!"

Minutes later, a weary doctor appeared at my bedside. There had been an emergency with another patient. They were short-staffed. Normally, there were two anesthesiologists on duty. He was very sorry.

"Turn on your side and hold still. Do not move," he said.

I turned and waited, gripping the bed rail, bracing myself for the mother-of-all shots.

I held my breath and closed my eyes.

Nothing.

Please, give me the shot, I pleaded in my head.

Nothing.

"Don't leave," I begged, sitting upright, as the doctor walked to the foot of the bed. "I *need* my epidural."

"I just gave it to you," he said, his kind, bloodshot eyes staring back at me. "Your pain will be gone in a few minutes. I won't leave you until your pain-free."

"Are you sure?" I asked, surprising myself with my question. He couldn't have given me the shot. Friends had warned me that the epidural hurt like hell. Some said it was worse than childbirth.

"Your contractions were coming so quickly that you couldn't feel it. You're going to get relief soon. Lie back down," he said, gently pushing my shoulders back against the hospital bed.

I was pain-free within five minutes.

A miracle.

His eyes are forever seared into my mind, along with his promise not to leave me until my pain was gone.

Doctor Stork (no joke) arrived in my room shortly after the anesthesiologist left.

"Ms. Quie, I'm sorry but we can't wait much longer for you to deliver. Your water broke over twelve hours ago. This baby needs to come out. We don't want to take any risks."

"That's fine," I said, relieved. I would have welcomed a cesarean way earlier.

"Good. I just put in an order for a C-section," she said with a smile, patting my legs as she left the room.

The next morning, I lay awake in my stiff hospital

bed watching a *Seinfeld* rerun while nine-pound William slept in the crook of my arm. Elaine just realized she'd revealed too much cleavage in her Christmas card. It was too late to do anything about it. The cards had already gone out. I found comfort in the predictable dynamics between the characters.

William was tightly wrapped in a blue-and-white-striped blanket, a light-blue cotton beanie nestled on his head. Every few minutes, I glanced in his direction.

"Hey, you," I'd say, looking for traces of myself in his tiny red face. Bill slept in a twin bed beside us.

Electricity jolted through my weary limbs. Shouldn't I feel tired? The nurses had already reprimanded me for not sleeping when William slept, but I couldn't. Once, I'd drifted off for a few minutes. I awoke to empty arms.

"Where's the baby?" I shouted, jolting up in bed, feeling for William on either side of me.

"What?" Bill asked, fumbling for his glasses on the table beside him.

"Where's the baby? Did he fall off the bed?" I asked, scanning the floor. I would have jumped out of bed, but the catheter reminded me to stay put.

"Hon, go back to sleep. A nurse came by and took him so you could rest. Don't you remember?" he asked, now standing beside the bed and resting his hand on mine. "You were wide awake."

My mind raced, trying to piece together his story. I vaguely remembered talking with a nurse. Hadn't she given me pain medicine for the cesarean? Did I really agree to let her take my baby? Why would I have done that?

"Oh God, I don't think she was wearing a name tag. What if she wasn't a real nurse?"

"This is crazy talk," Bill said, rolling his eyes at me. "You're just overtired."

"Go get the baby, Bill. I need him back."

We stared each other down. "This is nuts," Bill muttered as he left the room. Minutes later, he returned with our son and handed him over. I tucked him under my arm.

William's swollen eyes blinked open and stared into mine. This is the moment of a lifetime. Enjoy it, I told myself. I thought about all the mothers I'd seen on television holding their babies for the first time. They cried with elation. Why was I so afraid? He was just a baby. I loved babies. I wouldn't realize until months later that this panic was the beginning of my postpartum depression.

✳

About a week after the delivery, I awoke in a cold sweat with stabbing abdominal pain. When I couldn't get out of bed, Bill wanted to call an ambulance. I hated the idea of neighbors gawking at me in such a pathetic state. I slid out of bed and inched my way to the car, Bill at my side propping me up.

Mom, who was visiting from Baltimore, stayed behind with William, a mixture of concern and detachment on her face as I hobbled by her in the hallway. From what I could gather, she longed to be in Bill's position, caring for me. My allegiance was partially with her. That night, we both knew that my marriage had to come first.

The first doctor had me pee in a cup and sent me home with antibiotics for a urinary tract infection. We returned to the clinic the next morning after my fever shot up to 104 and I nearly fainted from the stomach pain. My knees shook as a new doctor conducted an excruciating pelvic exam that likely saved my life.

I had a severe uterine infection, a rare complication in some women who've labored well after their water breaks. The doctor instructed Bill to take me to the hospital immediately. Staff would be waiting. The baby could join us once I got settled.

Each day, doctors stopped by my room to fill me in on my rising white blood cell count. The current antibiotic had failed to control the infection. They would have to try another.

I was too sick to fret about my circumstances. My pain was less intense than childbirth but far worse than a migraine headache. Still, I refused pain medication. Despite my doctor's insistence that medication was safe to take while nursing, I didn't trust her. How could I, after my botched delivery? Sometimes, I'd give in: *Fine, I'll take the dumb medicine.*

Then the whole cycle started over.

By the end of my weeklong stay in the hospital, purple and green tracks lined my arms and dark circles rested beneath my eyes. I didn't just look like a junkie; I felt like one too. I had no appetite. I felt detached, as if I were watching myself. In a mere two weeks since the delivery, I'd dropped twenty-four of the twenty-eight pounds that I gained during the pregnancy.

On top of this, I sucked at nursing (no pun intended). The worst part was that even though William's mouth was clamped down on me like the Jaws of Life, the nurses only critiqued me. "Try to relax. That way, he won't have to strain so hard to feed," one suggested. Even the most seasoned lactation consultant had to use every trick in her giant toolbox to get William to nurse. "He's an impatient one," the lady said as she taped a tiny plastic tube to my chest. Once she enticed William to latch, she quickly pumped breast milk into his mouth to satisfy him. If the timing wasn't perfect, he'd scream as if we had taken a hammer to his toes.

The desperation I felt during William's early life is hard to describe. I'd never been so sick. I had to feed my baby but couldn't. Bill was always in the periphery; bringing me water, propping me up with a pillow, staring down at our son.

Once, after a particularly stressful nursing session, a nurse offered to mix up a packet of formula. "It's for newborns. It's full of vitamins."

"I'm not using formula," I said as if she'd offered my baby a bottle of gin. Weeks earlier, La Leche League had come to my Lamaze class. I had planned to nurse, but after their lecture, nursing was my only option. If he got sick and died, I couldn't live with myself. The fact that I got mastitis with accompanying high fevers, not once but four times, and couldn't keep up with William's enormous appetite was irrelevant. I had to provide my baby with the necessary antibodies to fight infection.

One doctor must have sensed my fragility. The night before I was discharged, she stood by my bedside, clipboard in hand.

"This is a sensitive time," she said, her kind eyes intent on mine. "You'll need to take special care of yourself when you get home. You've had far more stress than most new mothers."

I nodded and smiled, dismissing her comment. I'd counseled moms who could barely pay their bills.

"Some professional women like you struggle as new mothers. They're used to being in control. They don't know how to . . . how to let go. Parenthood is a different kind of journey. Try to relax. You'll enjoy it a lot more that way," she added, and then she slipped out the door.

I mulled over her words as William nursed in my arms. I glanced at the stack of parenting books that crowded my bedside table. My suitcase lay open against the wall, revealing perfectly folded pajamas, shorts, and T-shirts. My coping strategy for managing sticky situations—to organize the shit out of stuff—was embarrassingly transparent.

Persistence and attention to detail had served me well other times, like when I was twenty-nine, in graduate school, and pregnant with William. I had a terrible statistics teacher who closed his eyes in a euphoric state while he lectured. I tried to track his circuitous orations about coefficients and regression analyses, but none of it made sense. My classmates and I had stopped asking questions after the first week of class, when he reprimanded us that this was not an entry-level course.

As our first exam approached, I frantically searched for a tutor. Everyone I spoke to declined; they didn't teach doctoral-level statistics. Finally, a statistics student at the University of Washington referred me to Dr. Cunningham, a retired statistics professor.

After I got Dr. Cunningham on the phone and explained my predicament, he chuckled and invited me over. His wife had just made cookies for their grandchildren.

That semester, Dr. Cunningham and a few of my classmates spent hours at his kitchen table learning statistics—for free. I got a B in the class—a miracle. Dr. Cunningham even helped me analyze my data for my dissertation.

But as a new mother, my obsessive ways didn't serve me well. The harder I tried to master my new job, the more people reminded me to trust myself, to let go, to savor every moment with my baby.

I tried to follow their advice.

Boy, did I try.

I even started going to church. Bill called it my "woman church." Half the congregation was lesbian, the other half a mishmash of artsy yoga-types who compared their zodiac signs and gemstones during coffee hour. My therapist friend, Debbie, invited me after I broke down crying at her house on New Year's Eve. William was about four months old at the time.

"*Why* didn't you *tell* me you've been feeling like shit?" she asked, a hurt look on her face.

"I wanted to, Deb, but I didn't want to be a Debbie Downer," I said, wiping my tears with a grin. "You're so positive . . . and . . . so pregnant. I didn't want to freak you out."

Debbie pulled me in for a long hug. "Oh honey, don't worry about me," she said in her southern twang. "We've gotta stick together."

Debbie and I went to our "woman church" most Sundays. We listened to the spunky female minister's sermons about the power of self-love, generosity, and Buddhism. She raved about Sufi poets, like Rumi, who believed that the real sanctuary in life was within each of us. I dabbed my steady stream of tears, feeling half embarrassed and half relieved there was a place I could let my true feelings show.

Over time, relief overtook embarrassment. If Rumi felt I would settle into parenthood better by wearing gratitude as a cloak, I would try. I knew there was a lot to be thankful for. William was healthy, Bill was a loving husband and father, I had good friends, and I was keeping up in my doctoral studies in child psychology.

But by Sunday evening, my church high had worn off. Darkness crept back into my consciousness. I'd try to replace my fear and dread with gratitude, but I couldn't sustain it.

Looking back, if I had known that the usual onset of

postpartum depression (PPD) is one week to one month after delivery and that PPD should be suspected if the symptoms last more than two weeks, I would have been more assertive in getting more help. I had nearly all the symptoms: anxiety, insomnia, weight loss, crying episodes, hopelessness, guilt, and lack of concentration.

At the time, I thought I had the baby blues, a melancholy that many new mothers experience. Many of the parents I counseled in my practicum lived paycheck to paycheck. Some were on public assistance. *Their* lives were hard, not mine. I convinced myself that I didn't deserve to have PPD.

As I floundered, I tried to apply my main survival skills: work hard, exercise, keep your friends close, find humor in tough situations.

But panic infiltrated every cell in my body, especially at night. If I was lucky enough to drift off, I awoke several hours later with my heart pounding as if I were being chased to my death. Sometimes, when Bill got up to use the restroom, I'd scream. Bill shook me awake. You're okay, he said with his calm blue eyes and warm hands.

No, I'm not, I answered with my prolonged stare. I'm supposed to be enjoying my new baby. What's wrong with me?

Then came the panic attacks. I'd be giving William a bath or doing anything, really, and all of a sudden, my heart would pound, I'd be out of breath, and my hands would tingle. Tears usually followed, but not like normal. I didn't even feel them coming. I'd cuddle William close to my heart, drawing off his warmth, waiting for the wave to pass.

Then one morning at three, as I lay awake in the guest room by my new copy of *Myths about Insomnia*, I let my guard down long enough to accept the truth. My childhood dream of having the perfect family was crumbling. I had already listened to *Sacred Chants of Shiva* a gazillion times and my heart still pounded. Hard.

The next day, my voice shook as I asked one of my favorite professors for a referral to a psychologist. Doctoral students were encouraged to participate in therapy for personal growth, but my circumstances were different. I was losing my grip. I worried that my professor would regret letting me into the program or, even worse, limit my opportunities while in the program.

My professor smiled at me, commented on the universal stressors in graduate school, and offered me a chair in his office to talk. I politely declined. Baring my soul to a teacher just wasn't my style. I'd always been private about my personal life. He scribbled a few names and phone numbers on a piece of paper and offered his support whenever I needed it.

Counseling was nothing new to me. I'd seen psychologists off and on since childhood, mostly because my dad encouraged it. I think it made him feel better about his parenting foibles and my growing up without him in the home. Plus, I was the kind of kid who absorbed emotions around me. That was a lot to manage in a family with two hotheaded parents.

But as a doctoral student in child psychology, I wanted to help others, not have more counseling of my own. Bill didn't think I needed professional help, either. It wasn't the Norwegian way. He viewed therapy as a last-ditch option. If you were catatonic and peeing on yourself, then fine, go ahead, give therapy a try. Otherwise, stop dwelling on things you can't change and live your life.

Then, one Sunday morning when I got home from my woman church, Bill mentioned that a friend had asked about me.

"Who?" I asked as I slipped off my boots and hung up my winter coat.

"Doug," Bill answered as he fed William from a bottle.

"What'd he say?" I asked feeling my stomach swirl.

"That your arms look like toothpicks," Bill said, glancing up at me.

I looked down at my spindly arms covered in a long-sleeved shirt, then examined myself in the mirror. My cheeks were sunken. My arms resembled a ten-year-old child's. Doug was right.

"What'd you say?" I asked, as William pushed his bottle aside, smiled wide, and reached for me.

"I told him you were fine," Bill said, a crinkle in his brow.

"Do *you* think I'm fine?" I asked, bringing William in close for a kiss on the forehead.

"You're getting there. You're still a little wacky, but that's nothing new," he said with a smile.

As I rocked William in my lap, I pondered Bill's

denial. Normally, he was the kind of guy who pointed out the obvious. It was one of the things I loved about him.

I also considered our different reactions to parenthood. I had been ready for parenthood way before Bill. I practically had to force him to take the final leap.

"You're in your *mid*forties," I'd pressed when he insisted we weren't financially secure enough. Our fourteen-year age gap couldn't be ignored. I wanted at least two kids. They didn't all have to be biological, but we needed to get going.

But when William arrived, Bill embraced him wholeheartedly. He fussed over William, adjusting his blankets to make sure he wasn't too hot or too cold. He loved feeding him and even wanted William to sleep between us at night.

※

Dr. Lisa, the psychologist my professor recommended, was highly regarded in the psychoanalytic community in Seattle, an area I knew little about. I chose the health track during my second year of doctoral studies for a reason. I loved learning about the relationship between brain health and child development. It was complex and hopeful. With early intervention, many children could gain the skills to live satisfying lives. I found the children with developmental disorders endearing too. They disarmed me with their frank comments. I'd been so cautious as a child.

One of my professors, who specialized in neuropsychology, also encouraged me to follow my talent. He noticed my natural ability with writing and child assessment. I picked up on subtle nuances in children's language and behavior. Neuropsychology was an up-and-coming field. I would always have work.

Most of my classmates chose the clinical track. They teased me about my fixation with the frontal lobe, and I teased them about their fixations with the Oedipus complex. I couldn't deny that Freud had a few good points, especially as I reflected about my past and my surprisingly difficult adjustment to parenthood. Freud felt it was important to work through childhood conflicts to avoid transferring them to the next generation. This made sense. I didn't know if my postpartum depression was caused by my childhood stress, horrible birth with William, family genetics, or a combination, but I needed to get a grip. Truthfully, I just wanted to feel better. If psychoanalysis could help me get out from under the depression and panic attacks, I was in.

I saw Dr. Lisa for almost a year. I felt much better after each session. Even when I told her that I longed for my old life, she prompted me to explain and listened without judgment. When I told her that I'd only slept three hours the night before, she looked at me in amazement. She couldn't believe I'd showered and made it to counseling.

Sometimes, I brought William. Dr. Lisa noticed that I *was* bonded to William, a major feat in her eyes given my shaky upbringing and how crappy I'd felt since William was born. She pointed out little things, like the way William pulled his hands through my long hair and the way he smiled at me. She also noticed his intensity. He never napped in his car seat. If I didn't rotate his toys quickly, he fussed. He settled when I walked him in circles around her office.

Mostly, she validated my fatigue. She couldn't believe I wasn't on an antidepressant. I explained that I'd seen a handful of primary care doctors but none had recommended medication. The first suggested thirty minutes of daily exercise. The next swore by warm baths with Epsom salts in the evening. The third suggested that I drink a glass of wine with dinner. He also thought I should read *Myths about Insomnia,* a book by a Harvard doctor who promoted a drug-free, natural approach to treating sleep disorders. I followed their advice, but my mind still pinged from one fear to the next, like I was in a never-ending tightrope competition with no safety net.

I hadn't broached the subject of medication with doctors, either. I thought I'd have to quit nursing. I had no idea that some antidepressants were considered safe for nursing mothers.

Ultimately, I found a great psychiatrist, and after a few medication trials, he and I found the right mix. Within a few days, I could sleep, something I will never take for granted again.

A week or so later, the chronic lump in my throat melted away. Then food started to taste right. Bill says my sense of humor hasn't resumed pre-motherhood levels, but that's okay with me. I think I'm still pretty funny.

PEPS

When William was about six months old, my friend Kelly, who I met in Lamaze class, encouraged me to join a neighborhood moms group called Program for Early Parent Support (PEPS). With the counseling and medication, I was feeling much better, but I knew I could use the support.

I liked the other mothers from the start. We bonded over our new nightlife: Richard Simmons at two, British comedy at four, Viagra commercials. We laughed about our misconceptions of motherhood and how busy we thought we'd been in our twenties.

But the other babies pushed my buttons. How dare they crash on fuzzy blankets and let their mothers go solo to the bathroom? How could they sit in their car seats the entire hour?

Each week, I stood on the periphery of the group, swaying William in my arms. Sometimes, I could stop moving if I held him in front of a window. Then he could watch *others* move.

I wouldn't have resented the babies as much if William had slept better. In *What to Expect the First Year*, Arlene Eisenberg and Heidi Murkoff wrote that most babies slept fourteen to sixteen hours a day. William slept eight—nine on a good day.

His naps (we renamed them "snaps") consisted of fifteen-minute crashes in the backseat of the car. At dinner, even with the vibration mode activated in his Humpty

Dumpty bouncy seat, he squirmed, pinched up his face, and arched his back. Bill and I took turns bouncing him between bites. Then we walked him round and round our thousand-square-foot rambler. Usually, he'd nod off by ten o'clock, his chunky limbs splayed to the sides as if he'd been shot.

I felt betrayed. Why didn't anyone warn me that I'd be moving morning till night?

Bill was too cheery. "Think of it this way, hon," he'd say. "Since William doesn't need much sleep, he'll have more time for fun."

Are you kidding me? I thought. I'm not going to make it out of this parenting thing alive.

✳

Kelly gave me hope that I could make it through motherhood. I liked her no-nonsense personality and good attitude. She tied her long, dark hair into a high knot and threw on jeans, lip gloss, and flip-flops at a moment's notice. We bonded over our lack of sleep, breastfeeding fiascos, and food. Her baby was a terrible sleeper too.

On our walks around Greenlake, white elms, redwoods, and willow trees provided shade on hot summer days. The eccentric regulars touted their tight, muscular bodies in Speedos and bikinis. We giggled as we strolled our firstborns, now over a year old, around the lake.

Kelly and I had a thing for the magazine *Cooking Light*. I raved about the desserts, like Italian cream cake. She preferred entrees, like grilled portabella mushrooms with gorgonzola sauce.

"I don't get why people say they can't cook," she said one afternoon, breaking to a halt. "Who can't chop, measure, and mix? It's simple," she said, gripping her stroller handle, picking up speed again.

I agreed.

Whipping up Italian cream cake was nothing in comparison to parenting. My mom had described the first year of motherhood as "physically exhausting" given the diaper changes, nursing, and rocking. Even so, my mom friends seemed to have way more alone time than I did. They napped while their babies napped and put their babies to bed at seven.

My friend Jill's baby, Olivia, had the audacity to sleep sixteen hours a day. Jill even bragged about it on our evening strolls. It took everything I had not to ram her with my husky stroller when she complained about her nosy in-laws.

"What did they do?"

"They won't stop calling us. My mother-in-law acts like Olivia's *her* baby," she said, a look of disgust building on her well-rested face. "They want to watch her *every* Sunday. Paul works all week. *He* needs time with Olivia. She's *our* baby."

"Oh," I said. A nosy relative felt like a dream to me.

✳

Perplexed by William's quick gag reflex and finicky palate, I brought him to his metrosexual thirty-something pediatrician a handful of times.

"What's that?" one-year-old William would ask, pointing his chubby index finger to a minuscule brown speck on a plump, bright red strawberry. Unless the strawberry resembled one molded in a wax museum, William clamped his mouth shut and turned his face away.

Each visit, the doctor scrunched his brow, straightened his tie, and looked as bewildered as I did.

I always left with hollow advice: feed him a balanced diet of grains, fruits, vegetables, and small portions of meats and dairy but no bananas or white bread.

When I complained to my close friend Cara, a pediatrician, she laughed. "Pediatricians get shitty training on easy stuff like that."

Easy stuff? I thought. If it's so easy, why the hell can't I get my toddler to eat a strawberry?

The last time William and I trudged to the metrosexual, he offered a new suggestion: "Kids like their fruits and veggies sliced into cute shapes," he said with a half-smile.

When I stared him down, he extended himself. "Toothpicks and sauces make eating way more fun for toddlers."

I'd tried everything except the toothpicks.

Then I asked for a new pediatrician.

✳

Dr. Morris, the new doctor, shook his head and took a deep breath after we explained our predicament. In a nutshell, William refused all solid foods except pasta and parmesan cheese. Occasionally, we could get him to eat a few bites of a grilled cheese sandwich, no crust.

"He *must* eat fruits, vegetables, whole grains, and fiber daily," he said, as if Bill and I had banned William from roughage. "When children are hungry enough, they'll eat what they're given," he added, looking at me as if I were the problem. This was the first time he'd made eye contact with me. He wasn't especially polite to Bill either, but he acknowledged his presence.

I looked away. Who the hell did he think he was?

Before we left, Dr. Morris handed Bill a list of must-have groceries: pure pear juice, pure prune juice, raisins, and oatmeal.

As we walked toward the parking lot, my mind had a heyday casting spells on Dr. Morris. A flat tire on his way home from work, a vicious complaint to the medical board, a grandchild who only ate Pop-Tarts.

"What are you conjuring?" Bill asked, William in his arms.

"I've gone to the dark side. I'm having terrible thoughts," I said with a grin.

"The doctor says you need to eat fruits and vegetables," Bill lectured William as he strapped him into his car seat. "It's that simple."

William was too engrossed with his action figure to notice.

Inside, I knew my anger wasn't really about Dr. Morris, his shortsighted recommendations, or his attitude toward women.

I didn't know how to feed my son—monumental agony for a control freak and child professional. I should be able to tackle this problem myself. In my mind, if I worked hard enough with William, I could get him to eat. Children with bigger problems, like autism, got intensive services for "feeding difficulties." That wasn't my son.

But I listened hard when parents shared victories. Some got lucky with homemade renditions of applied behavior analysis (ABA), a Skinnerian behavioral reinforcement system. When a child swallowed a broccoli floret slathered in ranch dressing for an M&M, it gave me hope.

After our meeting with Dr. Morris, Bill and I drove to Whole Paycheck, our nickname for Whole Foods. We bought the most organic, perfect-looking white turkey meat we could find. Later, we stood side by side at the kitchen counter, slicing it into tiny square bites.

Once Bill and I had our minds set, we rounded up our materials: a bandana, a nose plug, and a bag of plain M&M's. Our goal was for him to eat one small bite of sliced turkey. To accomplish this, we needed to dull his acute olfactory and visual senses. William brought foods up to his nose, sniffed them three times, and gagged. He couldn't explain what he was sniffing for, but most foods didn't make the cut, especially fresh foods.

"Come here, buddy," I said, guilt rising in my body, as I buckled William into his booster seat and slid on the plastic tray. Who blindfolds their child to get him to eat? I thought.

The other part of my brain countered: Do it. He can't survive on bowtie noodles.

"Let's play a game where you try to guess what you're eating. It's sooo fun," I said, wrapping the red bandana around my head. "Where are you, William? I can't see you," I teased.

"I don't want to play."

"We've got really good treats, buddy," Bill added with a corny smile. "Do you want me to start? You can put food in my mouth and I'll try to guess what it is."

"No, Daddy. I don't want to play," William persisted, eyes filling with tears.

"Here's an M&M," I offered, breaking ABA rules. Who cares if he works for the chocolate?

"Mommy, I don't want to play. I want down," William cried, looking back and forth from Bill to me like we were aliens.

Bill and I stared at each other with disappointment. All of our work for nothing. What kid rejects M&M's?

"Okay," we resigned in unison, unstrapping his seat.

Neither of us was surprised that our homespun efforts at ABA had failed.

From the very beginning, William had only been easy in one area: sweetness.

The Lone Raisin

Before Bill served the oatmeal, he tucked a few raisins deep in the bottom of the bowl. "Breakfast is ready, William. Come here," he called, helping him into his booster seat. "This is the best kind of oatmeal," Bill bragged. "It's extra special."

"Oh my, that oatmeal looks so good!" I gushed, savoring a spoonful.

William stared back at us straight-faced, Bob the Builder spoon in hand. He dipped his spoon into the oatmeal, brought it to his nose and took a long sniff.

Please, just take a bite, I thought.

He brought the spoon to his mouth, closed his lips around it, and slowly swirled it around like a wine connoisseur tasting a two-hundred-dollar bottle of aged merlot.

Bill and I stood side by side like statues.

A second bite.

A third bite.

A fourth bite.

After the fifth bite, William's eyes narrowed, and a revolted expression grew across his face. Tears followed. Then came piercing, angry screams. William's mouth hung wide open like a baby bird, revealing the culprit: a lonely raisin that ruined it all.

Our dietary treatments had all failed. As I reached

42

in to unstrap him from his high chair, Bill shoved a fifth bite of oatmeal into William's gaping, trembling mouth.

What the hell are you doing? Are you crazy? I thought, giving Bill the look of death as William howled, flinging Bob the Builder to the ground.

Bill didn't care. He was done being stonewalled by his four-year-old.

PART TWO:
Moving to Minnesota

Here She Comes

"Take that, you lousy lowlife!" William ordered, clutching Apocalypse, his favorite action figure, in one hand and slicing the air with a pretend sword in the other. William wore navy sweatpants and an ultra-soft cotton T-shirt, his perma-outfit. He stood at the children's table of a coffee shop in Saint Paul, Minnesota, glaring at a mystery enemy across from him. "You're goin' downtown, mister!" he screeched, flinging Apocalypse over the table.

Bill's younger brother, David, had just picked us up at the airport. Bill, Dave, and I sipped coffee at a rustic pine table in the back corner. I was running on adrenaline after packing for the move most of the night. We'd purchased a home just four blocks from Bill's parents. We needed their help, especially with the baby on the way. We were months away from picking up our daughter from China.

For months, I had scanned job listings in Texas, Baltimore, and Minnesota, places we had family. I rarely saw anything of interest. Then a job listing caught my attention. A Minneapolis clinic needed a child psychologist with a specialization in neuropsychology. I'd just completed a fellowship in this area in Seattle.

Bill's cell phone rang, and he reached in his jacket pocket to answer it.

"Who is it?" I mouthed when we made eye contact. Bill shook his head, stood up, and walked to the table next to us. Seconds later, he walked to our table and handed me the phone.

"Hello Katherine, this is Karie from Americans Adopting Orphans," said a sweet voice on the other end. "We received your referral from China today."

"*Really?*" I said, suddenly standing. We weren't expecting the referral for at least three months, most likely six.

"*Yes*. Her picture is adorable. Her name is Pan Zi Xuan. I think you're going to be very happy. We'll send you the paperwork through certified mail this afternoon. Call us right away when you get it. We need to know if you accept the referral so that we can make arrangements. If you do, you'll travel with your group to China in two weeks."

My hands shook as I took in her words. In my thirty-four years, I'd never received a more life-altering phone call. We'd been matched with a baby, a daughter, after a process that had taken nearly two years.

I was thrilled, but we weren't ready. I'd just been hired for the position in Minneapolis and hadn't even started yet. At the interview, I didn't mention our adoption plans. I needed a job.

Before I hung up with Karie, I mustered one last question.

"How old is she?"

"She's fourteen months old, but she looks tiny," Karie answered, as if her smaller size buffered the reality that she'd spent a year or more in an orphanage. Baby girls in China are typically a few days old at the time of abandonment.

"Oh, thanks."

Like many other adoptive parents, I wanted an infant. The adoption process in China was painfully slow. China only allowed ten percent of babies in their orphanages to be adopted by foreigners. The chance of getting an infant was higher in other countries, like Korea, but Bill was over forty, the upper age limit. Still, my dream of adopting was finally coming true. I'd known I wanted to adopt since college. There was no particular trigger. Maybe it was my way of reassuring myself that I'd have children no matter what.

I couldn't wait to fly to China to meet her. I wondered if she would be healthy, mobile, timid, demanding. All these questions riffled through my mind as I pulled my emotions back to center.

Bill and David grinned at me as I rejoined them at the table. I put on a smile, sat down beside them, and took Bill's hand in mine. I would have to trust in our decision and enjoy the moment. If our daughter survived fourteen months in an orphanage, she could survive us.

"Looks like a celebration's happening at your house

tonight," said Dave, a smile burgeoning on his face. He was thirtysomething and single.

William ran over to us and pounced on David's lap. "Let's play samurai soldier at our new house, Uncle Dave, *please*," he begged. "I'm dyyying," William cried with a half-smile, dropping from Dave's lap onto the floor, one eye on Dave.

"Fine by me," I said, and Bill nodded along. No need to bring William in on the news about the baby until we accepted the referral.

Two days later, when I walked in the back door of our new house after work, I spotted a large white envelope with "Americans Adopting Orphans" written in bright red ink on the kitchen table. Adrenaline surged through my body. I paused and took a deep breath as I hung up my coat and pulled off my snow boots. Our daughter's history was finally within our grasp.

"Anyone home?" I yelled from the kitchen, listening for William and Bill.

Seconds later, I heard the clank of the fence in the backyard and spotted Bill coming up the walkway.

"Hey, hon," I said, pulling him into a squeeze, eyeing the big envelope. "Where's the little guy?"

"He's with the folks," Bill answered.

"I need a drink," I said, climbing onto our stool and searching above the fridge. "We've got Absolut, prosecco, Bloody Mary mix; what do you want?"

"How about one of each," Bill teased from the dining

room, picking out Waterford glasses from our built-in hutch.

I tucked the bottle of Absolut under my arm and jumped down, scanning the fridge for a mixer. I settled on cranberry juice.

We maneuvered around waist-height moving boxes and found an open spot on our couch. It was late October, and there was just enough light outside to see the huge oak tree in our front yard, mostly bare by now. Ellie, our toy poodle, jumped in my lap and curled into a tight ball.

Bill carefully opened the tightly sealed envelope and pulled out a large stack of paperwork. Near the bottom of the stack was a small, one-by-one-inch picture of Pan Zi Xuan stapled to the top right corner of a page. She was in a plain pink shirt, her dark hair cut short to the scalp, military style, her full lips pursed in a semi-frown. Her dark, piercing eyes made me shudder with self-doubt. Did I have what it took to care for a child who'd spent over a year in a Chinese orphanage?

"She's intense. Look at her eyes," I told Bill, who tugged at her picture trying to get the closer look.

"She's got a look, all right, like she's going to kill us in our sleep."

"*Hon*, don't ruin the moment. Don't call her an ax murderer."

"Can't you take a little joke? She's a baby. She's been living in an orphanage for over a year. What do you expect?"

Bill's question hit me. What did I expect? A cheerful,

chubby, bright-eyed baby? A daughter who'd been adored from day one, just like her brother? Was that so outlandish? Don't most mothers, adoptive or not, fantasize about having the perfect baby?

My mind skipped to William. How would he feel? When we'd asked if he wanted a sibling, he'd always said no. I'd brushed him off. What did he know? He was four.

My Texan dad was the worst. "Why Chiiina?" he'd asked when we told him our adoption plans. "What about William? The baby could have all *kiiinds* of troubles. It could ruin *William's liiife*. It could ruin *your liiife*. Who came up with this idea anyway?"

I refused to answer his questions. Who did he think he was, anyway? But although I wasn't ready to admit it, my dad's concern about a second child, specifically one who had spent over a year in a crowded orphanage, was one hundred percent valid. This baby would need so much more than I had imagined. I was notorious with friends and family for stretching myself too thin. I deluded myself that my background in child psychology would buffer us from the enormity of what we had taken on. Surely, my knowledge in child attachment and my love of children would pay off.

∗

I knew I needed to tell Bill about my adoption plans when we were dating. We had been living together in Seattle for almost a year. I hoped to marry him.

But I knew my adoption plan could be a deal-breaker. Most of my friends thought it was honorable but wouldn't consider it themselves; it was too risky.

After much consideration, I decided to tell Bill on a weekend camping trip in the Cascade Mountains, his happy place.

Our spoons clanked against metal bowls as Bill and I huddled together and devoured packets of peach and brown sugar Quaker instant oatmeal. "Don't you love the smell of pine?" Bill asked, taking a long whiff of the outdoors.

I inhaled and nodded with a smile. "It's beautiful up here," I answered, feeling my neck tighten.

"You tired?" Bill asked, taking my hand.

"No, just thinking."

"About what?" he asked.

"Adopting a baby," I said, breaking into nervous laughter.

"Adopting a *what?*" Bill asked, dropping my hand.

"*A baby*," I said, my heart pounding. "That's something I'm planning to do when I finish graduate school and get a real job someday."

"You mean you can't have kids?" Bill asked with a quizzical look.

"*No,* I want to have children *and* adopt a baby," I answered.

I knew I'd thrown Bill. He'd grown up with fewer surprises than me. His parents were two of the most levelheaded people I'd ever met. Bill set down his spoon, turned toward me, and paused. "You know you're crazy, right?" he asked with a grin.

"Yep."

"I guess I am too. I'm in," he said, taking my hand again.

We spent the next half hour bouncing around ideas about adoption as we packed up the campsite. Bill worried that if the child were from the United States, the biological parents could intervene. I worried about adopting from Russia given the higher levels of fetal alcohol syndrome in that part of the world. I hoped to adopt a child who'd lived in foster care, not an orphanage, the younger the better.

"What about China?" Bill asked an hour later, as we navigated our way down steep switchbacks. He explained that his father had traveled to China many times for work. As a doctor and professor, he'd been a guest lecturer to Chinese universities and hospitals.

"I'm in."

The Journey

"Put her down, Mommy. Let me look at her," four-year-old William said as we entered the front door. It was well past his bedtime, but we hadn't seen him in over two weeks. Bill and I had traveled for over twenty hours on our return from China. Mom and her husband John had come from Baltimore to stay with William while we were gone.

Mom gave me another long hug, kissed me on the cheek, and stared into my eyes, her routine whenever we'd been separated for a long stretch.

"Are you good?" she asked.

"Tired, filthy, the flight was hell," I said, scanning my dirty clothing.

Bill cleared a place next to William on the couch and slowly unwrapped our daughter, Emma Zi Quie. We'd hoped to keep her Chinese name, but as hard as we tried, we could never pronounce it correctly.

Emma was bound in an insanely expensive blanket we'd purchased in at the airport in Hong Kong. We had to throw the others away. Emma had been sick for over a day with a high fever, severe vomiting, and diarrhea, which worsened once we got to Hong Kong. We'd taken turns changing our clothing in the tiny airplane bathrooms. I'd even washed diarrhea out of my jeans pocket. We'd opened a bottle of perfume, another gift, on the flight and doused ourselves with it during bathroom breaks, trying to mask the smell. Everyone in our vicinity, from the burly military guy to the elegant Chinese elderly couple, nodded at us kindly as we troubleshot Emma's illness. The doctor who examined her in China had warned us that illness in newly adopted Chinese babies is very common. Babies rarely, if ever, left the orphanage. They hadn't built up immunities.

William sat cross-legged in his spot on the couch, his forehead pinched.

"Hurry, Dad. Lay her down. Is she cute?"

Bill rubbed Emma's back and eyed me, mulling over William's question.

The truth was, she wasn't that cute, not even in her Baby Gap lavender sweat suit. Her skin was a yellowish-green hue, her eyes runny, her body lean.

Two weeks earlier, when we met Emma in China, Bill and I had waited with thirty-plus adoptive parents in a cramped room, each of us shuffling through our paperwork, double- and triple-checking documents that would prove our identities. When our name was finally called, we were led down a hallway into another large room with a handful of babies and Chinese caretakers.

"Here you baby," an older woman said, pointing to a tiny toddler in her wobbly walker whose feet barely reached the floor. Emma had wispy black hair, a long neck, dark circles under her eyes, and a large scratch across her right cheek.

So here you are, I thought, comparing her to the tiny picture we'd received in the mail. Her steely eyes were now sunken. We've got to get you out of here. You need dumplings, tomato soup, mac and cheese.

Emma stared at me, then Bill.

"She you mama," the woman had said, crouching down beside Emma and pointing to me. "You hold her," she said, reaching for Emma.

"That's okay," I said, gesturing to the woman to let her stay put. I'd seen a handful of "gotcha day" videos where Chinese babies wailed when placed in their adoptive parents' arms. I wanted to take our time.

I felt like Emma was the CEO of a booming company and I was one of a thousand job applicants for a super important position: Mom.

Emma looked at me out of the corner of her eye, her mouth fixed in a straight line.

Would I make the cut?

*

"Hold on, buddy," I said to William, reaching for Emma, who lay against Bill's chest. "She's been really sick."

I slowly took Emma from Bill, turned her onto her back, and laid her down beside William.

Emma looked back at him, then at me, then Bill, sizing up her new life. Her jaw slacked. Then she smiled right at William, all gums. Bill had gotten her to laugh once at the hotel when he'd blown a loud kiss on her stomach, but she'd never smiled like this.

"She *is* cute," William said, taking her small, hot hands in his and examining her tiny fingernails.

Bill and I glanced at each other, overwhelmed by their reactions. We hadn't expected this.

Mom and John sat side by side and watched our new family unfold.

"What are these?" William asked, touching the bald spots on her head as Emma stared back at him.

"That's where doctors gave her medicine when she was sick in China. All of the babies in her orphanage got medicine that way," I answered, glancing at Mom, whose eyes widened.

"What's an orphanage?" William asked, scrunching his nose.

"A place where babies live until they find parents," I answered. I'd read books about adoption to William before, but he hadn't been interested.

"Where did her parents go?" he asked, dropping Emma's hand, climbing down from the couch into my lap.

"We don't know. I'll explain more tomorrow. Mommy's so tired right now, buddy. You need to get to bed too. I bet Daddy will lie down with you in your room and rub your back," I said, nudging Bill. He sat by me on the couch with Emma draped over his shoulder. When I looked closer, both of their eyes were closed.

"Are you her parents?" William asked, pointing at Bill, then me.

"Yes. We adopted her in China. She's your new little sister."

"Do you love her?"

"Yes, she's very sweet," I said, glancing up at Emma and Bill. Her arms hung at her sides, her breathing slow and steady.

"Do *I* love her?" William asked, staring up at Emma, then at me.

✳

Emma was nothing like William. While he chattered nonstop, she was silent. While he wandered up to strangers, she was panic-stricken.

Her stalker days began once we arrived in Minnesota. She kept a keen eye on me, waiting for me outside of the shower, clambering into my lap when I sat down, and throwing a tantrum if William sought the same comforts. It wasn't easy being stalked by a tiny, iron-willed toddler. Given her history and the hectic schedule we kept as a family, I tried not to hold a grudge.

Bill and I were thrilled when we learned of a Chinese-run day care in Saint Paul. All the staff were Chinese and spoke Mandarin to the children. They even served Chinese food for lunch. But unlike William, who glided into day care and preschool, Emma suffered.

When we arrived in the morning, Emma removed her shoes and coat slowly and deliberately. She looked at me longingly, as if she wanted to swallow me whole. At two, she needed us to commit to things beyond our capability. If our schedules changed and Bill greeted her with open arms instead of me, she wailed and kicked the back of his seat all the way home.

Emma had the same reaction when she awoke from a nap in the car. To avoid smashing into someone, I'd pull over on the side of the road to breathe. Stopping the car didn't halt the tantrum, but I could get some distance. Usually, I'd sit on the curb, hunched over and deflated, waiting her out.

This confused and disturbed strangers. "You need any help?" they'd ask, lingering.

"No thanks. We're fine," I'd answer with a forced smile, pushing back the tears.

William learned to stay out of Emma's way. Once, when he tried to give her a hug to calm her, she bit him hard on the nipple. At day care, she bit a child so hard on the ear that her parents found bloodstains on her pillow the next morning.

"I'm so sorry. We're working on it at home," I apologized when they confronted me at drop-off the next day. Most day cares wouldn't have tolerated Emma's antics, but her Chinese day care providers felt it was their obligation.

Adding to the stress was my choice of profession. During the day, I evaluated other people's children. At night, I managed my own. Bill had the night shift at his new job at Thomson Reuters as a reference attorney. There was no other option.

PART THREE:
Elementary School

You Think He Has What?

When I walked into the classroom, William's kindergarten teachers each smiled reflexively as if I were a surprise guest who'd shown up at their party. They sat at a round, orange, child-sized table. I sat down across from them like an oversized child in my tiny wooden chair, knees pressed up against the tabletop. It was near Thanksgiving. As I scanned the room, each child's self-portrait stared back at me.

William's teacher Julie was cordial, but her boundaries were firm, bordering on rigid. She wanted parents to wait outside of the classroom in the lobby at pickup time; she didn't like interruptions. Julie and her uncle, Mark, ran the preschool-kindergarten Montessori program. Mindy, the teaching assistant, had a round, youthful face and was quick to smile, mostly with her eyes. At conferences, it was standard for all three teachers to meet with parents. Still, it felt intimidating.

That afternoon, Julie sifted through her papers, straight-faced. Her dark brown hair was pulled back into a tight ponytail, revealing simple gold hoop earrings. Right before Julie spoke, she forced a smile. "We're glad you're here today," she said, taking a quick sip of coffee. "Before we get started, do you have any questions for us about William?"

I had questions, but I couldn't think of them. Why wasn't Julie commenting on the weather like usual? Since moving to Minnesota, I'd learned to appreciate weather talk. In the beginning, I thought it got in the way of real conversations. My eyes glazed over when neighbors spoke of northwest winds, precipitation, and snow flurries. But at work, I'd witnessed others use weather talk to glean information about parents' personalities, coping styles, and stress levels. If children and families were wound up, my colleagues spent more time on the weather. I'd adopted this strategy at work as a pediatric neuropsychologist too.

On this particular afternoon, even though it was deathly cold outside, I knew William's teachers and I were not going to chat about the windchill factor or black ice. I resented their strained faces, stirring up emotions I wasn't prepared for.

"I don't really have any questions. Is everything okay? You all look like someone just died," I said, shifting in my seat.

"We didn't mean to come across like that, but we have some concerns about William," Julie answered, restacking her paperwork. Her words resonated in my head as three worried faces stared back at me. I realized that I was about to be confronted head-on with news that my son's quirkiness might be something more serious.

Normally, Bill would have joined me at the conference. But days earlier, his great-uncle had unexpectedly passed away. The conference and funeral fell at the same time. When I'd called Julie to reschedule, she'd insisted that there were no other time slots available to meet, another sign of her rigidity. I felt bad about missing Uncle Leon's funeral, but Bill encouraged me to go to the conference.

"Tell me about your concerns," I forced out, rubbing my thumbs along the leather strap of my purse.

"William is a unique child who's doing well in many aspects of his development," she said, sitting up straighter in her chair. "But he's showing differences," she added, glancing to Mark and Mindy, an invitation to chime in. When they remained silent, she continued. "William gets confused with longer instructions. He can't learn routines. He's hard to reach, like he's in his own little world," she said, her eyes softening with each concern.

I stared back at her, my heart thumping in my chest. I'd had weekly contact with her for over a year now, but I couldn't warm up to her. Was it my denial about William's behavior that kept her at bay? My southern roots? Minnesota nice? I'd never lived in the Midwest before now. Whatever it was, that afternoon at conferences, I wanted none of her feedback.

"We think William should be evaluated by a professional," she said. "That way we can understand him better," she added with a smile as if her news were a good thing.

"Why didn't you all tell me any of this earlier in the school year?" I asked, feeling my cheeks redden. This was his second school conference. At the first, they hadn't given me reason for concern, or I hadn't interpreted their comments this way. They had described William as a sociable, happy child with a strong vocabulary. They said he needed reminders to complete his work but tempered this by mentioning that he was young.

Then, William had been demoted in the Thanksgiving play from a pilgrim to a turkey. His favorite part about being a pilgrim had been the toy musket they'd made out of papier-mâché in art class. Each evening, after we picked him up from school, he'd march from one end of the house to the other spouting weaponry facts, holding the musket firmly against his shoulder.

"Mommy, you want to hear something?" he'd asked one night, craning his round face into mine as I loaded the dishwasher. "My teacher John said pilgrims replaced matchlock muskets like mine with wheel lock guns. You want to know why?" he'd asked, clutching the gun against his chest as he circled me in the kitchen.

"Why?"

"Because the pilgrims had to light the matchlock's wick before they fired, so it if it was raining, they couldn't fire," he'd exclaimed, his eyes gleaming.

"Wow," I'd answered. Conversations with William were usually one-sided. Facts rarely stuck with me, yet they clung to him effortlessly.

About a week before the play, when I'd urged William to practice his lines, his eyes dropped to the floor.

"I'm not a pilgrim anymore," he'd said, glancing in my direction.

"What happened?" I'd asked, setting down my dish towel, trying to conceal my disappointment. If I hadn't been worried, I might not have been as affected by a demotion in a kindergarten play. But back then, I was always on alert. In my gut, I suspected he might have attention-deficit/hyperactivity disorder (ADHD), but when it came into my consciousness, I pushed it aside.

Other times, I worried that even more was going on. Given my background in child development, I couldn't ignore things that others might have seen as a blessing. When a mother at the park commented on William's booming language skills, I knew that precocious language development wasn't always a good thing. Children with certain disorders—like autism without intellectual impairment, formerly referred to as Asperger's disorder—often have advanced language development, resembling little professors.

William had sensory differences, too. He would only wear soft sweatpants and T-shirts—his "comfy cozies." The tags in his clothing had to be cut off. He resisted most foods. He covered his ears when he heard innocuous sounds, like a toilet flushing.

Like most parents, even though I knew something wasn't right, I held out hope that I was wrong. I reminded myself of his strengths. He made great eye contact, smiled readily, craved interaction and physical contact, commented on others' emotions, and adorned himself in Bob the Builder bright yellow goggles and work belts.

That day when William shared about his demotion, I pulled him into my lap and listened to his side of the story.

"They had too many pilgrims and not enough turkeys," he said, hopping down. Unless I had a stack of books, I couldn't hold his attention for more than a few seconds.

When I had called Mark for an explanation the next day, he chalked it up to William's missed rehearsal when we were out of town. As much as I wanted to believe him, I didn't buy it.

Everything required so much effort with William. Unless I took him by the hand, sat him down on the staircase, and put something in his hands to occupy him, I couldn't get his shoes on. He'd stand back up and wander in another direction. How could Mark get him to act in a school play?

*

Julie, William's kindergarten teacher, moved her hands along the stack of papers, her security blanket.

"We would have mentioned it to you last fall, but we wanted to give William time. He hasn't matured like we would expect. He's showing what we call 'uneven development,'" she said, glancing up at me. "His vocabulary is off the charts, but he can't write his name, stay with the group, or put his shoes on the right feet." She paused and smiled sympathetically, the way people do before they give you more bad news. "William reminds me a lot of my youngest son. He was recently diagnosed with a form of autism."

Tears welled in my eyes as I took in her words. I routinely told parents not to be frightened by autism. It was only a word that described a combination of symptoms. Now, as a mother, I was daunted by the possibility of my child having an autism-spectrum disorder. I had witnessed the roller coaster of emotions parents of autistic children endured. They each grieved for unexpected losses: their child had never been invited to a birthday party, they couldn't go out to dinner because of embarrassing tantrums, they hadn't had a full night's sleep in years. Instead of enrolling their child in neighborhood activities, like basketball and hockey, their afternoons were spent driving to therapies, often miles away.

At work, I was good at guiding parents whose children had special needs. My experience as a mother helped me understand a lot of what they were going through. But I had no interest in joining them. Their lives were too hard. I'd grown up in a chaotic family. I convinced myself that

Bill and I could sidestep professional support for William if we worked extra hard with him.

Mark reached over and placed a box of Kleenex in front of me. I pulled a few tissues from the box, stared at my hands, and wadded them into a tight ball, a conscious effort to pull myself together. Even though William had attended the school for nearly a year, I rarely interacted with Mark. He was quiet and shy with adults yet exuded a calming presence with children. Sometimes, if I arrived early for pickup, I could see him sitting in the corner of the room surrounded by a small ring of kindergartners enthralled by his lesson. He passed around hand-sized models of dwellings, hunting tools, and foods. He brought history to life for his students.

"William is very lucky to have you as a mother. He really is," said Mark.

When I looked up to thank him, I was caught off guard. He was on the verge of tears. I don't remember if I thanked him. After Julie mentioned autism, my brain reached maximum capacity. Thoughts came to me, but I couldn't decode them.

"Thank you for your feedback about William," I said, glancing up at each teacher as I gathered my coat and scarf, which hung on the back of my tiny chair.

Mark offered to get the door.

"No, thanks. I'm good," I said, opening the heavy glass door to the freezing winter air.

A New Reality

After the school conference, I drifted from the classroom to my car, to our house. When I pulled into the driveway and put the car into park, I looked into the rearview mirror and scanned my face. Did the new me, the me who'd been forced out of denial, look different?

Oh God. I looked like shit.

Streaks of mascara ran down each side of my pink, splotchy face. I scrubbed the black makeup off with my shirtsleeve and ran a powder brush across my face.

Pull yourself together. Breathe. No one's dying here, I told myself, relaxing my shoulders away from my ears. As I walked along the flagstone path to our back door, I peered into the bay window. William was standing at the kitchen table face-to-face with his clunky Buzz Lightyear doll, a favorite since his second birthday. Bill was at the stove. I didn't see Emma.

"Hi, Momma," William said, peering out the back door, reaching for my hand as I came up the steps. "Daddy's making pasta. Do you want some?"

"Hi, sweet boy," I said, pulling William into a tight squeeze. "I'll eat later. I need to lie down," I said, forcing a smile, running my fingers through his thick blond hair. At times like this, William seemed like any other five-year-old. He smiled, laughed, played with his action figures, shared about his day, and sought me out for affection. That's what made accepting his teachers' feedback so hard.

"Hi, hon," Bill said from the stove, a cloud of steam rising from the pot. He'd changed out of the black suit he'd worn to Uncle Leon's funeral and into sweats and a T-shirt.

"Hi," I said, trying my best to keep my voice steady as I hung up my coat and pulled off my boots. Usually, I talked to Bill from the minute I got home, running through the events from the day.

Emma, now two, sat on the floor by Ellie. She walked toward me, her arms out wide, a mixture of excitement and frustration on her face. "Mama," she said, wrapping her arms around me, burying her head in my legs. Unlike William, who was hefty at two, Emma was tiny. I could lift her with one arm.

"You okay, hon?" Bill asked, eyeing me suspiciously.

"I just need to lie down. I've got a killer headache. I want to hear about the funeral, just not now," I answered, feeling the constriction in my throat, holding back another wave of tears. "Sorry I can't help out. Let's connect in a few minutes," I said, tucking a wisp of Emma's jet-black hair behind her ear before I passed her off to Bill.

Upstairs, I pulled off my wool sweater and cords, drew the white shades, and crawled into our pine four-poster bed. The cool sheets and heavy down comforter felt good against my skin. Our bedroom was my sanctuary. Bill teased me about how I called it *my* room, but it was one of the only places I felt relaxed. A few months earlier, I'd painted it a light, dusty bluish-green that reminded me of the ocean. The white, double-hung windows resembled those of my childhood home. My father had given me the pine bed for my sixteenth birthday.

When I closed my eyes, I heard Bill in the living room reasoning with William. Emma was silent, her norm. My mind flashed back to the very beginning with William.

Seemingly simple things, like hair washing, triggered intense crying episodes.

"I don't like this," William would say, clutching me in fear as if I were ditching him in the ocean. "Ahhh! It's touching my face," he would scream, writhing out of Bill's grip, scrambling for me to pick him up, his hair full of soap.

Sometimes, I picked him up anyway. "We tried. I can't take it anymore," I reassured Bill as I dried William off.

I never knew what caused him to shake in terror when he got even the tiniest speck of water on his face. We adjusted the temperature, bought softer washcloths, and dimmed the lighting. None of it seemed to matter.

Emma was entirely different. When her face got wet, she blinked her eyes wide and smiled at us.

I heard Bill creak up the stairs, open Emma's bedroom door, and pull up the side rail of her crib. Unlike William, she never protested naps. I knew that children like Emma who'd spent time in orphanages needed to learn to depend on others. Still, her ability to fall asleep and play on her own felt heavenly. We'd taken on too much. I had to let some things go.

Bill opened our door a crack and peered in. I looked up, wishing I could pull the blankets over my head and erase the last hour from my memory.

"What happened at the conference?" he asked, scooching me over, sandwiching my hand between his.

"They think he should be evaluated," I said, taking comfort in the warmth of his hands.

"Why?"

"Because he's not developing like the other kids," I answered, tracing the lines in Bill's palm, twice the size of mine, wishing I could predict the future.

"In what way?" Bill asked, as if we'd never discussed William's troubles.

"Lot of ways, hon," I said, pulling him down beside me on his side of the bed, resting my head on his chest. "They notice the same things we do; that he can't stop moving, that he can't follow directions," I said as Bill rubbed my back. "They even mentioned autism," I added, scanning Bill's face for a reaction.

"Really?" Don't autistic kids keep to themselves? We can't get William out of our face," he said with a grin. I couldn't help but smile back.

"I don't know. I'm the wrong one to ask. I was blown away today. I'm clearly in serious denial."

"You're nutty, but you're not clueless," Bill added with another smile.

"Psychologists are notorious for being nutty

parents," I answered, burying my face in a pillow. As we bantered, I tried to piece the puzzle together. Had my hellish delivery with William damaged his brain? Or was it our genetics? Bill and I each had creative, eccentric relatives who fit the description of adult ADHD. Whatever it was, Bill's calming presence gave me hope that we could face the next steps together.

Kindergarten, Round Two

Bill and I sat in his old kindergarten classroom elbow-to-elbow with fifty other nervous parents. Bill had attended kindergarten in the same space, a few blocks from his childhood home. We sifted through brightly colored forms lit up by fluorescent lighting. An industrial fan spun hot air throughout the room as the backs of my legs stuck to the fiberglass chair.

William's new kindergarten teacher, Ms. Jones, looked to be in her late twenties.

"Starting kindergarten is a big step for parents and children. It's normal to worry," she said, her face softening as she scanned ours. "This is my eighth year of teaching. I promise to take good care of your children. I'll distract them when they miss you, help them make friends, and prepare them for first grade," she added with a smile.

All of this sounded good to me. I felt my shoulders relax. I glanced at Bill, who stared straight ahead. I had no idea what he was thinking.

"One thing you can do to improve your child's experience is give them a quick hug and leave after the bell rings," Ms. Jones said with a half-smile. "Hanging around makes life more difficult for your child and for me."

I was equally floored and impressed by Ms. Jones's sense of authority and confidence, foreign to me in my twenties. Her presence calmed my nerves and gave me hope that the new school year would be better than the last.

Bill fidgeted in his seat and wrung his hands.

"What's the matter?" I asked.

"I always forget how sick I feel in schools," Bill answered, massaging his forehead and looking at the ground as if he might throw up.

"Do you need to leave?" I asked, half worried, half frustrated. I felt for him, but on Parent Information Night, two weeks before William started his second year of kindergarten, I had enough to worry about. At six, William could barely write his name.

Bill nodded his head, his eyes still focused on his feet. I flashed back to a conversation we had years earlier when we first met.

"What did you read growing up?" I'd asked with a smile, recalling Amelia Bedelia dressing a chicken in tiny clothing.

"Nothing much," he'd answered with a shrug.

"Can't you think of *one* favorite childhood book?" I'd teased. My mind flooded with fond memories of Babar, Eloise, and her pug Weenie.

Bill had paused, set down his beer, and sat back in his chair.

"I couldn't read," he'd answered.

His words had hung in the air.

"What?"

"People learn by patterns," he'd explained, tracing the corners of his coaster with his forefinger. "I couldn't see the patterns. Letters meant nothing to me."

It had been hard to believe. Bill had gone to law school. When I studied for the GRE, he could define words like garrulous.

"How did you learn?"

Bill had explained that, in first grade, he learned to vomit on command at his desk. It happened so often that his teacher sent him to the nurse's office without looking up from her work. In second grade, after he was diagnosed with dyslexia, his parents pulled him from public school and enrolled him in a private school. He'd had tutoring after school too.

＊

A few days after Parent Information Night, I contacted Ms. Jones through email. I explained that William's last teachers expressed concern about his difficulty following directions. I asked her to contact me if she noticed anything out of the ordinary. At the time, I felt that if I gave her more information, I would influence her views of William. I wanted her to form her own perceptions.

"Thanks for being in touch," she responded. "If I notice anything concerning, I'll contact you right away. I look forward to meeting your family."

The next week, I walked William to school. The weather was perfect: warm but not hot, a thin layer of haze lifting already, revealing patches of light blue sky. I'd dropped Emma, now three, at my in-laws' earlier that morning before Bill left for work.

I found comfort in our light conversation and William's slow stroll. It took us over half an hour to walk three blocks, but I didn't care. I worked four ten-hour days conducting neuropsychological evaluations with children. By Friday, my day off, my mind was shot. Meandering with a six-year-old was just my speed.

"Would you want to be Hermione or Harry?" William asked, wielding a stick at me as if he were casting a spell. He wore his favorite outfit: navy sweats, Keds tennis shoes, and a soft cotton T-shirt. I caught a glimpse of grape jelly on his cheek and wiped it with my thumb.

"Hmmm. It's hard to say. Maybe I'd be Hermione since she was a super smart Muggle girl."

At times like this, William seemed like any other six-year-old. He whirled his stick left and right, stabbing his imaginary enemy.

"Watch where you're going," I warned as he ran behind me, narrowly missing bumps in the sidewalk that would have sent him flying. Once something caught William's interest, he couldn't break away to check his surroundings, even if it jeopardized his safety. He'd fallen so many times as a toddler that Bill had considered getting him a helmet.

As we neared school, a throng of other parents, mostly mothers, came into view. Many of their faces were familiar from my weekly trips to Speedy, the local grocery store. Still, we rarely exchanged words. I'd tried to strike up a conversation a few times, but it fell flat. How hard is it to smile? I thought. I don't bite.

Prior to moving to Minnesota, I had gathered friends as effortlessly as one gathers inches around the waist in middle age. But we had been in Saint Paul for two years now, and I still had no social life outside my husband's family.

"What the hell is wrong with me?" I'd asked Bill one night, half laughing and half crying, as I climbed into bed.

"You're too nice," he'd said, wrapping his arms around me.

"Too nice?" I'd asked. "*I smile.* Is something wrong with that?"

"Just relax, hon. Midwesterners aren't like Texans. You guys are super social; we take our time."

✳

When the morning bell rang, kindergarteners clung to their mothers, who huddled in a mob outside of Ms. Jones's classroom door. William unlocked his warm hand from mine and waved goodbye. Separating from me was second nature. He'd never known life with a stay-at-home mother.

Mothers chatted loudly amongst themselves in the hallway. Conversation centered around kitchen remodels, older siblings' homework, and clueless husbands. I stood and watched from the sidelines, half wishing I were part of their group. They seemed to have all the time in the world. Suddenly, the classroom door opened. Ms. Jones eyed the women in the hallway and pulled her door hard with a thud.

The next week, when I picked William up from school, instead of shooing me away, Ms. Jones waved me down as if she were signaling a cab driver to pull over. I felt a familiar surge of anxiety in the pit of my stomach and braced myself for more bad news.

"Ms. Quie, do you have a few minutes?" she asked as I helped William gather his belongings by his locker.

"Sure, where should we meet?" I answered, reminding myself to breathe. My good friend Gwen, an occupational therapist, swore by belly breathing.

"Let's meet in my classroom," said Ms. Jones.

"Okay, I'll be right there," I answered, walking William to the playground. He spotted a friend straddling the lower branch of a towering oak tree and scurried after him.

As I pulled open the heavy doors to the building and headed toward Ms. Jones's classroom, I told myself that, regardless of what she said, I could take it. How bad could it be anyway? I hated feeling like a scared rabbit.

Ms. Jones explained that William talked "constantly" in class. She wondered if he were like this at home.

"Yes," I answered, relieved that even his spunky teacher found his talking exhausting. I couldn't block it out like Bill.

"*Really?* His talking is so intense. How do you deal with it?" she asked, her eyes widening.

At that moment, the look of disbelief on Ms. Jones's face, coupled with my own skyrocketing anxiety, triggered a nervous burst of laughter. If I hadn't laughed, I might have cried. More than one neighbor had described Ms. Jones as the most laid-back kindergarten teacher at school.

"His talking drives me crazy too," I said, cracking up. "It's exhausting. I haven't found a perfect solution."

Ms. Jones smiled. "Any ideas?" she asked, pen in hand.

I contemplated the list of strategies I suggested to parents of hyperactive kids at work and those Bill and I had used with William at home. I'd read nearly all Russell Barkley's research-based books about ADHD. He had studied ADHD for thirty-plus years. His books were dry but packed with information about how to help children and families affected by ADHD.

I was packed with knowledge about ADHD too. But at that moment, as I tried to help Ms. Jones manage William, my mind moved in slow motion, bogged down by fear of what was to come. It reminded me that the tough years of raising William were not behind us.

Then a few strategies came to mind: "It helps if you kneel down beside him, make physical contact, and give him something to hold." From my work at the office, I'd learned that when I gave kids with ADHD something to hold, it slowed their bodies down, including their need to talk.

Ms. Jones wrote quickly in her spiral notebook and nodded along, hanging on my every word. "Thank you for your help," she said, massaging one of her temples. "My normal classroom system isn't working with William. I've had him stand on the yellow think-spot in the classroom every day now. Usually, it helps students learn to control their bodies better, but with William, it doesn't have any effect."

As I took in Ms. Jones's words, I tried to stay calm. William hadn't mentioned any of this at home, but his excitement about kindergarten had waned. I was reminded of a picture I'd found on the kitchen table near William's pile of action figures. It was a stick figure drawn in pencil on yellow legal paper. I'd picked it up and scanned it. William rarely drew, but I'd recognized his rudimentary work. The figure floated on the page above a large circle. He'd drawn a straight line for the mouth. When I had asked him about it, he'd mentioned something about "standing on think." I had thought nothing of it. For all I knew, *think* was a planet in his fantasy solar system.

Ms. Jones and I agreed to talk with William

separately about the plan. I thanked her and headed out to the playground.

As William skidded down the slide, my eyes met his and I forced a smile. He knew I had been talking to his teacher.

Emma

At the office, I didn't take kids' behavior personally. When a child hurled blocks at me, I understood. They had their own problems.

With Emma, I felt responsible. Bill and I brought her to the United States. During the adoption process, we signed documents promising to love and care for our daughter. There were rumors that Americans wanted Chinese children as servants. I worried that her life would have been better with a stay-at-home mom. Most of the adoptive mothers we met in China planned to stay home for at least a year. But I needed to work full-time. Even if I were making more money, there weren't part-time jobs for pediatric neuropsychologists.

During Emma's first year, I tried to remember the advice I'd received from the adoption agency: keep life simple, set limits with friends and family, let the baby bond with you first, wear her in a sling for added close-ness so that she feels secure. Pre-adoption, all of this seemed logical. What parent wouldn't make simple sacri-fices for their anxious toddler?

Post-adoption, this advice felt like a cruel joke.

Nothing about our life was simple.

At six, William still needed help getting his shoes on. The littlest thing brought him off course. He couldn't resist an action figure on the stairwell or himself in the mirror.

But he was happy. In the mornings, on the way to Discovery Club, he tapped his feet and sang along to the music. He even recognized artists.

"Is this the sad lady that sounds like a man?" he asked when I played my Tracy Chapman album.

At nearly two, Emma was a wiz at self-care. She pulled her hair into tiny ponytails and effortlessly maneuvered zippers and buttons. Her skin color had finally lost the greenish hue. She no longer had bald spots from poor nutrition and lying on her back in the orphanage. She'd grown into clothing for a one-year-old. On the outside, she was thriving.

On the inside, we were barely scratching the surface. She still clung to me, especially in the mornings before we went our separate ways. I rationalized my intensive work schedule by telling myself that Emma was getting far more love and attention in our family than she would have received in China.

I was sick of following societal norms too. I'd grown up in the South, where the underlying message was that women should stay home and support their man. My aunt had assumed that I would drop out of graduate school when William was born. Nobody had asked Bill or my male colleagues if they were planning to quit their jobs. The few months Bill had stayed home with the kids after we moved to Minnesota, he'd likened it to being at the bottom of a swimming pool, slowly drowning to death. Emma didn't give a rip about my feminist streak. She wanted me home.

"Emma, it's cold outside. You *have* to wear socks," I said, preparing for battle every morning. Then, she grabbed the toe of her sock, looked up at me, and yanked it off. Her Chinese day care providers wrapped the children in thick layers of clothing when they went to the outdoor playground, even after the snow thawed. I hated their disapproving looks when Emma arrived barefoot.

"Nope, you're wearing socks," I said, pulling her into my lap on the stairwell as she shrieked and tried to get away. My hands shook with frustration as I reached for her tiny feet. Huge tears ran down Emma's cheeks.

William watched on with his hands over his ears.

"Emma, put your socks on," he said, resting her sock on the stairs, stepping back.

I glanced at the clock. I had to drop William at Discovery Club and Emma at day care before my nine o'clock evaluation. Parents waited months for an appointment.

"Fine, grab your boots," I said, releasing Emma. I gathered my briefcase and the kids' backpacks. Emma toddled behind me, barefoot, her face splotchy and tired.

"Come on, William," I barked.

When I arrived at the office, my heart was in my

throat. I tried to breathe, relax my shoulders, visualize a crimson sunset at the cabin.

Nothing helped.

I felt like a fraud. How could I help children and parents get to the root of their problems if I were barely squeaking by?

Now that Emma was here, I worried about William. I visualized him covering his ears as she screamed in the backseat of the car, at the kitchen table, at the grocery store. William had told me more than once that he was afraid of Emma.

I'd consider scheduling an appointment with a child psychologist. Then she'd show tiny signs of improvement and I'd put it off. Instead of sitting rigid in my arms, she'd rest her head on my shoulder.

✳

"I need help with my daughter. We did our home study with you," I explained to the receptionist at Children's Home Society one morning.

"Sure," the woman said, handing me a sheet of paper. I scanned the page from top to bottom. Social workers, licensed psychologists, and marriage and family therapists filled the page. I had no idea who to choose. I could have asked someone at work, but I didn't trust myself to have a conversation without sobbing.

Marga and I met a week later. Her dark hair was pulled back into a low ponytail. She wore a loose-fitting skirt and blouse and no makeup. Her office was deco-rated with colorful Guatemalan artwork. Photographs of children from all over the world covered one wall. A doll-house sat in the corner. Due to our opposite schedules, Bill was still at work.

"What brought you here?" Marga asked, her hands in her lap, leaning toward me.

"I'm so overwhelmed," I said, reaching for the Kleenex on the coffee table. I hadn't been in a therapist's office since my insomnia was at its peak when William was a baby. Why had I waited so long? Emma was nearly three years old. She'd been with us for over six months.

I told Marga that Emma's cry was so angry and shrill that it rattled my brain. Instead of drawing me to her, it repelled me. I explained that Emma was so jealous of William that she'd bite him when he got too close to me. I told Marga that life was so hard that I doubted my decision to adopt. I didn't like attachment parenting techniques, at least the ones I'd read about. I wasn't the touchy-feely type who welcomed a family bed. I needed my own space.

Marga smiled knowingly. "Emma's had a tough be-ginning, but she's resilient," she explained, taking a sip of her water on the coffee table. "Emma can handle your limits. She needs to understand you're in charge. That will help her feel secure," she added, leaning toward me. "Parenting comes in all shapes and sizes. You have to be yourself. Children sense it if you're trying to be some-thing you're not."

"Really?" I asked, letting her words soak in.

"*Yes*. Give her a short time-out if you need to. She'll survive. She has to mold to *your* life too. You have what it takes to parent Emma. You wouldn't have done it otherwise. Adoptive parents are a unique breed."

I drove home from our meeting renewed. I didn't have to force myself into an adoptive parent mold that blocked my air supply. I could still be me. I'd always been independent. It was no coincidence that I'd fallen in love with a Norwegian who'd seriously thought he might end up a bachelor.

When I got home from the therapy session, Bill had already put both kids to bed. William wasn't asleep yet. I could hear him flipping the pages of his books, mumbling to himself. Eventually, he collapsed into sleep.

"How was it?" Bill asked as I changed into my favorite soft cotton pajamas.

"I like her. I'm going back next week," I answered, patting cool face cream across my forehead and cheeks.

"Really?" he asked, tucking another pillow behind his head.

"Yeah. It just helps to talk to someone who understands. She could probably help us with William too."

Bill nodded and lay his head back down on his pillow.

"I want you to come with me," I said, climbing into bed.

"Me?" he asked, pointing to his chest. "You don't need me," he said with a sheepish smile.

"I do too," I said, raising my eyebrows at him.

I Want to Stop, but I Can't

"Can we talk?" Ms. Jones asked a few days later as William and I walked to his classroom. She explained that the suggestions I'd given had helped some, but William was still distracting to other students. It was hard to teach.

"Sure," I said, giving William a quick hug and sending him on his way. We quickly schemed a plan for the day. That evening, as William walked in circles around the kitchen table, Bill and I talked with him about the importance of listening in class. He needed to look at Ms. Jones when she was talking and *zip it*.

"You can pick out *any* action figure you want at Target on Friday after school if you stay quiet," we explained.

William stopped pacing and scanned our faces. "I *want* to stop talking, but I *can't*," he said.

Bill and I stared back at him with surprise. He knew his limits better than we did, even back then.

A few days later, Ms. Jones spotted me in the hallway and waved me down, her brow crinkled. She explained that after lunch, she walked by the bathroom and heard some kids talking in there. She knocked on the door to ask them to finish up. Then William walked out alone.

"So he'd been talking to himself?" I asked.

"Yes," she said, shaking her head. "I think he went in the bathroom because he couldn't stop talking in the classroom. I've never had a student do that," she added, taking a breath. "I think you should have him evaluated."

Her words resonated in my head, joining phrases from his Montessori teachers.

When Bill returned from work that evening, the kids were nonresponsive in the living room, immersed in *Toy Story* for the umpteenth time.

"*Don't eat.* Dinner's almost ready," I said, tugging Bill away from the fridge.

"Aren't you the little drill sergeant," he retorted, pulling me into a hug.

The lump in my throat that had formed during my conversation with Ms. Jones now hurt. I knew that if I looked at Bill, tears would follow.

"What is it?" Bill asked, one hand on my waist, tipping my chin upward with the other, forcing eye contact.

"Nothing new," I answered. "It's just hard," I added, searching the fridge for shredded cheese and sour cream.

"Is it William?"

"Yes," I answered, cleaver in hand, dicing green onion and cilantro to smithereens. "I was going to tell you after the kids went to bed, but I can't hold it in."

"What happened? Did he get kicked out of school?" he asked, a half grin on his face.

"Why are you smiling? It's not funny. His teacher is concerned. She told me that William was talking to himself in the bathroom at school today."

"That's kind of funny. Don't you think?" Bill asked from the kitchen table, pulling off his shoes.

"Bill, we can't ignore it this time. We need to get him evaluated," I said as I set the kids' plastic monkey plates across from each other at the table.

Bill looked at me, this time without a smile. "It seems like everybody's getting pretty worked up over a kid being a kid."

"I don't see how it can hurt to have him tested," I said, trying to reassure us both. The assessment could potentially change the course of his life. I didn't want him labeled, either. But we needed help.

I'd have to trust in the process. Diagnosis or not, he'd be the same little boy I'd loved from the very beginning.

✳

Bill navigated through rush-hour traffic to Minneapolis on Highway 94, tapping his thumbs against the steering wheel to Stevie Ray Vaughan, keeping a steady beat.

Normally, when I wasn't going to the office, I wore sweats and a hoodie. That morning, I dressed in black slacks and my favorite coral sweater. Growing up, my mother insisted that we dress nicely for appointments. "If everything goes to hell, at least you'll look good," she laughed.

The waiting room at Children's Hospital was stark. Clunky wooden chairs lined the walls, a bucket of Legos sat in the corner, and children's books were piled in a mound on a rickety coffee table. William sat cross-legged on the floor and scooped Legos into his lap.

Bill and I kept our eyes on him, smiling reflexively when he looked up from play. For the first time, I realized what it was like for the parents of children I evaluated. I felt vulnerable and jittery. As much as I wanted Dr. Smith's opinion, I also feared it. So much was at stake.

When Dr. Smith rounded the corner, he knelt down by William, smiled, and extended his hand for a shake. He looked my age, midthirties. He wore dark blue jeans, a button-down oxford shirt, and a red Mickey Mouse tie. William shook his hand, smiled, and stood up, Legos splattering across the linoleum floor.

"Nice to meet you," Dr. Smith said, shaking our hands, as we all huddled on the floor, cleaning up the Legos. "This way," he said, signaling for us to follow him down a narrow hallway. "William, grab a few toys to play with in the hallway while I meet with your parents in my office," he directed, pointing to a wicker basket in his office and then to a small play area outside of his door.

As William headed for the basket, a wooden figurine at the top of Dr. Smith's bookshelf caught his eye. Then he swiftly anchored one foot on the shelf and scaled the bookcase, Spider-Man style, reaching high for the figurine. Normally, we would have plucked him off the shelf fast. That day, we watched with a mixture of horror that our son was literally climbing the psychologist's walls and relief that Dr. Smith was there to see it.

"You're a good climber," Dr. Smith said with a smile. "It's not breakable. You can play with it in the hallway," he said to William, who gave no reaction. He was too intent on twisting the figurine's limbs.

"Are you kidding me, William?" Bill chided, leading him by the hand to the hallway. "Climbing the doctor's bookcase, William, *really*? Don't do that again."

"Okay," he answered without expression, setting up the new toys on his hands and knees. The wooden figurine stood to the right of him, abandoned after the conquest.

Dr. Smith sat back in his chair and leafed through the packet of paperwork we had mailed in weeks earlier in preparation for our appointment. His office was small, dominated by a ceiling-high bookcase full of thick neuropsychology books and sprinkled with models of brains: one with neon-colored regions, one flesh-colored and spongy, another wrought-iron, a modern sculpture.

"I've read through all of your paperwork. It looks like you're mostly concerned about William's difficulty focusing and some hyperactivity. Is that still true? Has anything changed over the last few months?" he asked.

I looked at Bill to see if he wanted to answer, and he stared back without a word—my cue to start. "Those are still our main concerns," I said, not wanting to speak for Bill. "Do you have anything you want to add, hon?" I asked Bill, who sat stiffly beside me in his chair.

"No," he answered, like a stranger. I'd forgotten how aloof he became at doctor's visits. When we'd discussed it in the past, he'd explained that when I tried to bring him into these discussions, he felt I was putting him on the spot; if he had something to share, he'd say it. Still, I didn't understand the change in his personality around professionals. I chalked it up to his anxiety about our son. It left me feeling alone in navigating William's care.

"Is there anything in particular you're wondering about?" the doctor asked.

"ADHD," I said, rubbing my fingers along my smooth bangle bracelets.

"Okay. How long have you been concerned?" he asked, skimming our paperwork. "Since his first year of kindergarten?" he answered, once he got to the page where we'd listed our concerns.

"Earlier, when William was four, he and I visited my dad in Texas. One night, after I'd finally gotten William to bed, Dad told me was worried about him."

"He did?" Bill interjected, glancing at me with surprise.

"Yeah, don't you remember? I told you about it when we got back."

"No," he answered, sitting back in his seat and chewing the end of his pen.

"Well, he did. We'd only been there a day. William had talked through the entire baseball game, all the way back to the car, all the way home—you get the idea. That night, Dad said, 'Honey, something's wrong with that boy. He's either manic or off-the-charts ADHD.' I'd suspected something was wrong, but that's when I knew."

Unlike Bill's parents, Dad didn't mince words. When he'd commented on William's behavior that weekend, it had come as a relief; maybe my exhaustion from parenting William was warranted.

"Do you see signs of mania in him?" Dr. Smith asked, flipping through our paperwork, scribbling notes. As professionals, we usually spoke in layman's terms, but I knew what he meant. He wondered if William was pressured, irritable, quick to rage.

"No, he's a happy kid. That's why I think it may be ADHD. But my dad has bipolar I disorder," I answered, softening my voice as if *bipolar*, a mental health condition characterized by major depressive episodes and mania, were a bad word. I rarely mentioned Dad's diagnosis. It felt too personal, as if I were revealing something about him that others would misunderstand.

Dad's illness didn't conjure good memories, either. During depressive episodes, he stayed in bed, barely ate, and lost his best quality—humor. At the other extreme, when Dad was manic, he barely slept, laughed too much, and stared so intensely that it made me nervous.

Dr. Smith jotted a few words on his notepad. "Anything else you want me to look at?" he asked, looking back and forth between us.

"Learning. William struggles to write his name and to recognize letters and numbers. There's a family history of dyslexia," I answered, glancing over at Bill.

"He loves to be read to, though," Bill added.

"That's true. He does love that," I said, smiling at Bill. I knew his dyslexia embarrassed him.

"Okay. Do you all have other questions about the testing process?" he asked, standing behind his desk.

"No, I think we're good," I answered, gathering my purse and paperwork. The packet of information we received in the mail described the testing process in detail. Plus, I had heard great things about Dr. Smith from a few colleagues who were excellent psychologists.

"See you later, buddy," Bill said, leaning down to pat William on the back. He had built a rectangular fort out of blocks, and was sprawled out on his stomach peering inside, oblivious to us.

As we left the office, I felt thankful we'd scheduled the testing with Dr. Smith. He was a natural with kids. He could handle William.

I thought about the stark contrast in our children too. At four, Emma hid behind me at doctor's appointments. I would have felt terrible leaving her with anyone unfamiliar.

What Is Coding?

As Bill and I drove to Children's Hospital on the day of the feedback session two weeks later, I tried to make sense of my worries. None of this was new. I'd suspected William had ADHD since he was three or four years old. We'd already survived it for six years. ADHD wasn't life threatening.

But I knew that if William received a formal diagnosis of ADHD, we could no longer pretend that he was a late bloomer, that he would grow out of whatever it was that made things so difficult. A diagnosis like ADHD would change his future, the way others felt about him, the way he felt about himself.

Bill and I barely spoke as we walked to the pediatric neuropsychology clinic. As we sat down in the waiting room, I tried to occupy myself with a cooking magazine. Everything was stuffed with Miracle Whip, so I put it down.

This time, when Dr. Smith rounded the corner, he wore a bright green Kermit the Frog tie.

"Come on back. Let's talk about your son."

We sat down in his office, and he handed us each a copy of William's report. At least five minutes passed while Bill and I scanned the information.

"What's 'coding'?'" Bill asked, chewing the end of his pen, pointing to William's lowest score, in the 5th percentile for his age.

I wasn't surprised that William bombed coding, but I was curious to hear Dr. Smith's explanation.

"It's a subtest from an IQ test that measures visual processing speed. Kids with lower coding scores have difficulty tracking visual information, writing things down, and completing written work at a typical pace," Dr. Smith answered, sipping his coffee.

"What does it mean for *my kid?*" Bill asked, his eyes narrow, leaning back in his seat.

"It means that William may need more time to complete written work. Taking notes from the board may be hard because it requires him to transfer information from one place to another."

"Is it permanent?" Bill asked, his forehead scrunched.

"Not necessarily. Children's brains change a lot over time. His processing speed could improve quite a bit as he develops." I knew this, but still, it was a relief to hear it from Dr. Smith. "If you all don't mind, I'd like to shift our focus for a minute. I think it would be more helpful if I explained the results from a big-picture standpoint. Then we can put all of the information together."

"Sure."

"William's language skills are very strong, at the 99th percentile for his age. He could define words like 'ancient' and 'transparent.' He even knew what 'foresight' meant. That's unusual for a six-year-old," he said with a smile. "This could explain some of his difficulty focusing. He's probably bored in kindergarten, particularly since he's repeating it this year."

"He's talked for five years straight," I said with a smile. "He should have strong language skills."

"It's true," Bill added, giving his first hint of a smile.

This helped take the edge off for me. I mulled Dr. Smith's comments over in my head, trying to make sense of them. As much as I wanted to believe that William's kindergarten troubles were rooted in giftedness, it still didn't explain why he needed so many reminders to do simple things like brushing his teeth. It didn't explain his constant movement either.

"William's visual reasoning skills are strong too—86th percentile," he added with a smile. "He could replicate block designs and complete visual patterns easily. Kids who do well in visual reasoning often excel in subjects like geometry. He could grow up to be an architect or a pilot."

"A pilot? Are you sure you're looking at the right test results?" Bill asked, a grin building on his face. "I don't care how smart he looks on paper, he's a maniac. You saw him climb your bookcase," he teased.

"Let's talk about that," Dr. Smith said turning more serious. "The questionnaire from his kindergarten teacher suggests that William has a hard time paying attention and sitting still; so do your parent ratings."

Dr. Smith laid out the blue questionnaire Ms. Jones had completed and mailed in for the appointment. My eyes scanned the page from top to bottom:

Often leaves seat

Needs a lot of supervision

Needs reminders to keep hands to self

Talks excessively

Daydreams

Is easily distracted by sights or sounds

Has difficulty getting started or persisting in tasks

Spelling is poor

Is forgetful in daily activities

Next to each trait was a scale from zero, meaning it was not at all applicable to William, to three, meaning it was a significant problem. Ms. Jones had circled threes for many items. "Hmm. That's not so good," I said.

"William was pretty active during testing too," he said. "Lower scores in processing speed are common in children with ADHD. It's hard for these kids to shift from one task or thought quickly. Some research suggests that kids with ADHD focus fine. They just have difficulty shifting focus."

"So what are you trying to say? Does he have ADHD or not?" Bill asked, sitting back in his chair.

"I've given his testing a lot of thought. William shows many signs of ADHD, but his higher IQ complicates things. Gifted kids learn differently. They need to be more challenged than your average kindergartener. Easy concepts don't hold their attention well. I'd like to make the diagnosis of ADHD, not otherwise specified, for now. In the field, it's referred to as ADHD-NOS."

"ADHD *what*?" Bill interrupted.

"*Hon,* can you hold on a minute and let the guy talk?" I asked, putting my hand on his knee. "This is what I deal with all the time," I teased, smiling at Dr. Smith and shaking my head.

"What? I'm not doing anything," Bill replied with a knowing smile, the one he made when he was cornered in an argument.

"No problem. This diagnosis stuff is confusing," he said. "ADHD-NOS means that while William has many symptoms of ADHD, they don't fit neatly into a specific ADHD category, like the inattentive type or the hyperactive-impulsive type. Because of his intelligence and younger age, I'd like to wait and see how William develops over the next year or so. If he keeps struggling with inattention, hyperactivity, and impulsivity, he'll meet criteria for ADHD, combined type. Does that help?"

"What should we do in the meantime, when he's driving his teacher crazy? How do you treat ADHD?" Bill asked, rubbing his knees.

"Good question," Dr. Smith answered, leaning forward in his seat, scribbling on a piece of paper. "There are a few options. School supports—like having William sit near his teacher in the classroom, take movement breaks throughout the school day, and get extra help with reading and writing—tend to be helpful. If those supports aren't enough, medication is another option," he said, scanning our faces.

"Thanks," Bill said, checking his watch. "I'm hoping Ms. Jones can work some magic in the classroom. I'd rather not tranquilize him unless we have to," he added, moving to a standing position.

I wasn't thrilled to put William on medication either, but I realized the seriousness of our situation. Repeating kindergarten a third time was not an option.

No More Gifts, Please

William chose a Harry Potter theme for his seventh

birthday. It was fall, and the weather in Saint Paul was perfect. Our towering oak tree in the backyard provided shade, a home for the kids' newly built tree house, and sturdy branches for swings, all pluses for an outdoor party. Bill and I bought dry ice for the witch's brew and sticks, straw, and twine for broom-making.

"Do you want me to write down his gifts for him?" my friend Jana asked, always one step ahead of me.

"Can you write his thank-you notes too?" I teased, trying to fight the knot growing in my stomach. William had made it through his second year of kindergarten, but it was touch-and-go. Ms. Jones and I strategized weekly. We reviewed Dr. Smith's evaluation together and did our best to put his recommendations into action: William should sit near Ms. Jones during circle time. Access to "fidgets," like Silly Putty, could help him to stay seated and listen better. Praise was the key to promoting positive behaviors, not punishment. Daily reward systems should be used. If "environmental supports" like these weren't successful, he recommended medication.

I could remember the times I sat at the kitchen table during elementary school, a stack of blank notes beside me. Mom stood nearby in the kitchen, coaching me on different ways to express thanks. I dreaded those notes. School hadn't even been an obstacle for me.

At William's party, I eyeballed the mound of gifts covering the picnic table on our deck. Twelve presents? How was that possible? There were eleven guests. Who had the nerve to bring more than one? That meant, including family, we had at least sixteen notes to write.

William sat in a large deck chair surrounded by his friends, their energy mounting. He'd invited eleven boys and one girl, a hockey player; think Peppermint Patty from Peanuts, freckles and all. Bill had taken Emma to his parents'.

"Open mine first!"

"William, open mine!"

They chanted and jumped up and down, straddling their makeshift brooms.

I glanced at Jana. I was used to working with one child at a time. She was a kindergarten teacher.

Jana stood up and walked toward the back door. "Okay everyone, eyes on me. We're drawing numbers, one to twelve. Come pick them out of my hand," she said. "William's opening presents in that order."

Everyone quickly lined up. I sat back and let Jana do her magic. She was the first good friend I had made in Minnesota. We met earlier that school year at a school potluck. Her son was in William's kindergarten class.

William was all smiles in his shimmery, black-and-hunter-green cape, navy sweats, and a plain black T-shirt. He ripped open Harry Potter Lego sets, a wooden shield, and hefty picture books full of mythical creatures.

"Thanks, Marc . . . Thanks, Maria . . . Thanks, George," he said, a broad smile on his face.

I was full of gratitude. This was his first birthday party in Minnesota.

A week after his birthday, I mustered the strength to help William tackle his thank-you notes.

"Just write, 'Dear Granny,'" I instructed, pointing to the blank note on the kitchen table. "All you have to do is copy what I've written for you right here."

William's eyes bounced from me to the note and then back to Bill as if they were pulled by an invisible hand. Bill didn't understand why I felt compelled to seek Mom's approval even though I lived miles away from her judgment. I tried to adopt my mother-in-law's nonjudgmental attitude like a new outfit, but it felt like I was playing dress-up in someone else's wardrobe.

"Think about it this way, hon," Bill interrupted. "The people who blacklist William for not sending them thank-you notes are off our list too. Then we'll never have to talk to them again," he said with a grin.

"It's not that simple, Bill," I said, glaring at him. "People expect moms to teach their kids manners," I said. "They never blame dads. You're off the hook."

"Fine, whatever you say," Bill said, walking away, hands up.

Minutes later, when William wandered away from the table again, I wrote the note for him. I could hear Mom: "You know, Kath, kids these days have really lost their manners. Boys were always given the easy way out when I was a kid. I hope you don't do that with William. If you do everything for him, he'll never learn to be independent."

The next day, when William returned from school, I

vowed to hold him accountable. He could copy two short notes a day.

"William, Granddad and Mimi gave you the *Dragonology* book. Copy what I've written on this paper," I said, placing a pencil in his right hand.

DEaR GRan, William wrote, his tongue thrust to the side, revealing his immense effort.

"Mommy, did you know that Jabba the Hutt is the crime boss?" he asked, jumping out of his chair, rocking side to side, right foot, left foot. "He wants Hans Solo's head. Isn't he fat and ugly?" he asked, staring into my eyes, his nose scrunched up in disgust.

"Yeah, he's super ugly, but we can talk about Jabba later. We've got to finish this note."

"Okay," he agreed, his forehead pinched. "Mom, I need to sharpen my pencil," he said seconds later, darting across the room, hands rifling through the utility drawer in search of his skull-and-crossbones sharpener. "Mom! I found my fuzzy man in here! I've missed him," he said, grazing the two-inch-tall, bright yellow troll doll across his cheek.

"William, get back here! You've written one and a half words in ten minutes."

William fumbled in his pocket, pulled out a small, glittery bouncy ball, and dribbled it beside him.

"Put the ball back in your pocket William."

"Look how high it bounces, Mom," he said, pointing high at the sparkly sphere as it grazed the ceiling.

"William, I'm not joking around. I'm losing my

patience with you," I said, feeling my neck tighten. "Hand me the ball," I said, thrusting my open palm at him.

"Just one more time, Mom," he said, a grin on his face.

"GIVE ME THE BALL!" I yelled, snatching it from him. "All I want you to do is *copy* two sentences! *Two sentences*. I don't get it. What am I doing wrong?" I screamed. The blank note stared back at me, mocking my failure.

William covered his face and peeked through his fingers at me. I could see the outline of his mouth turned downward in a perfect frown. His feet thumped lightly against the chair, the rest of him frozen.

"William, how can I help you write?" I asked. I'd seen samples of William's writing at school conferences. He wrote like a preschooler, with pressure in large print, causing the muscles in his small hands to cramp and spasm in pain. He intermixed capital and lowercase letters and reversed his *b*'s and *d*'s. Somehow, with my help, I'd expected his writing problems to disappear, like a headache after taking Tylenol.

"I don't know," he answered from behind his hands. "My brain just hates these notes for some reason." William fanned his fingers wider, revealing his blue eyes.

On a rational level, I knew that William's ADHD and writing difficulties were not my fault. I could logically trace his problems to genetics. But as a new mother, guilt crept into my psyche. During William's early years, guilt tried to convince me that I had *caused* his ADHD. If I had monitored him more closely, he wouldn't have fallen off the deck and smacked his forehead as a toddler, damaging his frontal lobe. If I had been more diligent with my prenatal vitamins, he wouldn't have been as susceptible to ADHD.

I witnessed this same blame game with the mothers I counseled at work. They tearfully divulged their "sins": a glass of wine or piece of sushi during pregnancy. Like me, they wondered if they had caused their child's problems. The answer was almost always a simple no. On the contrary, most mothers of kids with developmental differences are fiercely selfless women. Their purses brim with clementines, juice boxes, and string cheese. They carry binders packed with testing records, medication lists, and special education documents.

Back then, I was lousy at kicking guilt to the curb. It's taken a long time, but I'm getting better at telling guilt to look elsewhere when it tries to lecture me on my inadequacies. I try to remember one of my favorite Rumi sayings to help set myself free: The art of knowing, is knowing what to ignore.

Ms. Smith

As I drove to the house, I focused on my breathing. Breathe in positive energy, breathe out things you can't change.

I felt rattled from my work at Fairview Riverside Hospital on the children's inpatient mental health unit.

For over an hour, a ten-year-old boy with curly blond hair had paced back and forth across a long rectangular table in the testing area while I tried to break into his world. A psychiatrist had referred him for testing in hopes that I could help with treatment planning. I had given up on cognitive testing quickly, as he couldn't stop moving, much less concentrate on my questions. Just a few days earlier, he had tried to jump out of his parents' car on the highway.

It was late September, and the air had already turned chilly in Saint Paul. Our dutch elm and oak trees were nearly bare, which made me appreciate the row of arborvitae Bill had planted along our fence. William had been in first grade for a few weeks now. Emma was now attending Chinese preschool.

Emma peeked her head out of the back door, phone in hand. "For you, Mama."

"Hi, Emma," I said, relieved to be home. Life with Emma had been easier since we'd begun counseling with Marga. Bill no longer worked the night shift as a reference attorney, either, which made evenings with the kids less stressful.

"Are you eating dinner? I can call you back," my neighbor Nancy offered when I picked up the phone. Our boys had the same teacher.

"I just walked in the door, Nancy. What's up?" I asked, smiling at Bill, who had set the table and prepared his standard dinner: spaghetti and salad. I could hear William playing with his action figures in the basement, his favorite spot.

"Do you know anything about this prize the kids are trying to earn in Ms. Smith's class?"

Are you serious? I thought. You're calling me about a class prize? How would I know? I couldn't help but resent Nancy's stay-at-home life after my long day.

"I don't know, Nancy. I'll check with William later. He hasn't mentioned anything," I said, pulling Emma into my lap.

"Thanks. Mark's super frustrated. He says Ms. Smith has promised the kids a reward, but they keep missing out on it."

At that moment, I had a sinking feeling that William had something to do with Mark's frustration. Mark was a serious rule-follower. I'll never know for sure, but I suspected Nancy's plan had been to alert me, in her own subtle Minnesota way, that William was holding the class back.

After dinner, as William paged through his Incredible Hulk book in the living room, transfixed by his favorite green giant, I sat down on the couch beside him.

"Hey, buddy, can I ask you something?"

"Huh?" he answered, eyes glued to the page.

"Are you working on getting a reward in your class with Ms. Smith?"

"Yeah," he responded after he flipped the page a few seconds later.

"What do you have to do to get the reward?"

No response.

"Hey, buddy. I need to talk to you," I said, slipping the book out of his hands.

Conversations with William felt like wading through a vat of quicksand. This fit with the research of Russell Barkley, a world-renowned ADHD specialist. He found that kids with ADHD can actually focus on their interests better than typical kids. The struggle is in shifting from one thing to the next. "Can you look at me?"

"Uh-huh," he answered, picking up a Star Wars clone trooper on the coffee table.

"What do you have to do to get the reward in your class?" I asked, waiting for an answer, as he fitted the trooper's gun into his holster. "William, what do you have to do to get the reward in your class?" I repeated, turning his face toward mine.

"Something good," he said, maneuvering around me so he could pull the trooper's gun out of his ammunition belt and position it in his tiny hands, preparing to fire.

"Like what?" I pressed, fantasizing about locking him in a padded room with nothing but the two of us in it. "Let me hold onto your stormtrooper," I said, taking it out of his hands. "It's hard to talk to you when you're playing with him. William, what do you need to do to get the reward in your class?"

"You have to be quiet and raise your hand," he answered slowly, now mesmerized by a string at the seam of his T-shirt.

"What happens when kids talk?" I asked, holding William's hands, hoping to shift him off the string. Now that I had his hands, his eyes danced around the room restlessly, searching for their new target. Over the years, I had learned that if I wanted William's attention, it helped to apply deep pressure, like a firm hug. I squeezed and massaged his hands. Then he looked right at me.

"Ms. Smith puts your name on the board."

"Whose name gets put on the board?"

"I don't know," he answered, eyes cruising the room.

"Does Ben's?"

"No."

"Does Ellen's?"

"No."

"Does Sean's?"

"No."

"Does yours?"

"Yes," William answered, glancing at me briefly, scanning my face for a reaction.

I was good at staying calm with other people's children. Maintaining a carefree facial expression with my own children was far more challenging. The minute I heard phrases like, "I was sent to the think spot," my insides turned. That day, I was on a special mission. I had to keep my emotions in check. If I showed too much of a reaction, William would hold back vital information I needed to help him.

"How many days a week does your name get on the board?"

"I don't know."

"One, two, three, four, or five days," I asked, holding up corresponding fingers.

"Maybe four."

"What happens when someone's name gets on the board?"

"They can't have playtime on Fridays or get the prize Ms. Smith is saving for us."

"What happens during playtime?"

"You can play games with your friends or read."

"What do the kids who get their names on the board do during playtime?"

"We have to put our heads down on our desks," William answered, looking down.

I visualized William laying his head down on his desk while twenty-four of his classmates played Sorry, Connect 4, and Uno beside him. Why hadn't he told us about this? Did he think we'd punish him? Did he think he deserved it?

Deep down, I suspected he didn't want to see the disappointment in my eyes or listen to the long lecture he knew would follow. I was tired of listening to my lectures too. Talking with William made no difference. He agreed: sitting in his seat was good; talking out of turn was bad. He just couldn't make good on the deal.

"I'm sorry, buddy," I sympathized. "That doesn't sound fun at all." I sat in silence on the couch beside William, rubbing his back, taking in the enormity of his comment, as he squeezed a throw pillow in his lap. William rarely complained of school woes. He preferred conversation about fun stuff, like songs he and his best friend Sean made up at school.

As I contemplated our next move, William slid

from the couch to the floor and crawled across the rug to his beloved pile of action figures. He sifted through them carefully in search of his two favorite guys. His face lit up with a wicked grin when he'd achieved his mission.

The ninja action figure in his right hand threatened the ogre in his left. "Why, I oughta slice you to ribbons, you dirty scoundrel. You want a piece of me?"

"Yeah, I'm going to take you down. You're going downtown!" the ogre retorted, jumping on Ninja's back. They broke into a full battle, rolling back and forth across the rug, as William's small hands wielded them in all directions.

I sifted through my CDs, trying to contain the litany of negative thoughts running through my head. I spotted Janis Joplin and clicked to one of my favorite songs, "Me and Bobby McGee." I envisioned myself on a road trip with my closest friends in college without a care in the world.

Fun Friday

Each Friday, when I picked William up from after-school care, I scanned his face for a clue. Had he finally made it to Fun Friday? I could never tell. He rarely recounted details of the day.

One Friday at dinner, I carefully broached the subject while Bill and the kids settled in at the table. Emma, now four, rarely spoke at dinner. For her, mealtime was a competition. She expended her energy monitoring how many bowtie noodles and broccoli florets William got. She'd been with us for over three years, but her fear of not getting enough lingered. She ate twice as much as William.

"Did you guys have a party today?" I asked William, reaching for his hand to give it a pat, my way of getting his attention.

"Yeah," he answered, pulling Boba Fett from his pocket, one of his favorite action figures.

"How was it?" I asked, serving Emma more noodles.

"Fine," he answered with a smile, flipping Boba Fett's brown cape to the side.

"Did you go?"

"No."

"You want to talk about it?" I hated grilling William, but Fun Friday was my main barometer for his behavior at school.

"No," he said, tipping back in his seat.

Bill and I exchanged glances and shrugged. Emma looked up from her plate and scanned our faces as if she were preparing to endure another lecture to William.

"You two can be excused," I said. By now, I knew lectures were pointless.

I consoled myself with dark humor as I washed the dishes. "I could send her hate mail," I told Bill, who sat at the kitchen table polishing off a pint of Ben and Jerry's Cherry Garcia.

"What would you write?" he asked with a smile.

"How about this: Dear Ms. Smith, this is a letter from the party committee in your neighborhood. We regret to inform you that you may no longer participate in Sensational Saturday," I said, cracking a smile as I dried my hands with a dish towel.

"Perfect."

That night, I tossed and turned in bed. Bashing Ms. Smith helped me let off steam, but it didn't change our son's predicament. I knew she wasn't a horrible person. She was trying to teach William life lessons: you must take your schoolwork seriously; work first, then play at Fun Friday; if you don't follow the rules, you can't run with the rest of the pack.

The next day, Bill and I scheduled an afternoon meeting with Ms. Smith. It was late October, and the weather outside was turning cold. Nearly all of the trees had been stripped of their leaves, reminding me that the harsh winter was approaching. When we arrived at her classroom, Ms. Smith motioned for us to come in and sit down across from her. A stiff, starched white collar revealed itself around her neckline, decorated with a small gold cross necklace.

Everything about Ms. Smith's appearance and classroom was neat and tidy. Even the pencils on her desk were sharpened like mini spears, lined up military style, standing up for attention. Colored sticky notes on her desk revealed impeccable handwriting. No wonder our son drove her nuts. While Ms. Smith moved in a linear, organized fashion, William zigzagged erratically, overflowing with random comments, extraneous movements, smudged papers, broken pencils, miscalculated math problems, and backward letters.

Ms. Smith started the meeting by commenting on the cooler weather.

Bill sat upright in his seat, kneading his hands together on the table, and forced a smile. "William tells me you have some kind of system in your classroom where kids are working toward a reward. Can you tell me more about this?" he asked.

"Sure," she answered. "Since school started, we've been working toward a class party. In order to earn the party, all the kids have to work together to follow classroom rules."

"Hmm. What are the rules?" Bill asked.

"They're pretty basic. The children have to stay quiet during lesson time, ask permission to leave their seats, treat each other with respect, and be good listeners."

"So what happens if a student breaks one of your rules?" Bill asked, sitting back in his chair, lightly crossing his arms.

"Good question," she answered, shifting in her seat, breaking eye contact with him. "If one of my students misbehaves, I write their name on the board."

"Why?" he asked, reflexively.

"It helps students learn to take accountability for their behavior. They learn that their behavior impacts others. It's an important life lesson. I've used this reward system for years. It helps children work together as a group and become a cohesive unit," she explained.

"But I thought you said you didn't think William could control his talking?" I blurted. Ms. Smith had sent me an email earlier in the school year saying that she had given William a time-out for talking during the lesson. She had mentioned that he had begun to sing "It Ain't Gonna Rain No More" with his hands over his mouth during his time-out. At the very end of her email, she commented that she wasn't sure if he could help it.

I couldn't help but smile when she mentioned what he was singing that day. I had no idea where William heard that song, but it touched him. When he sang the line, "Now my baby's gone," he held the word *gone* and shook his head side to side, as if he could see his lady walking away.

"William may have more difficulty controlling his behavior than many of his classmates, but I haven't had to make exceptions for other students in the past. We shouldn't lower our expectations for him. William needs to know that we believe in him."

By the intense look in Bill's eyes and the flushed color of his cheeks, I could tell he had waited too long to speak his mind.

"Wait a minute. You mean you're telling me that if William interrupts somebody or gets up and walks around without permission, the whole class suffers as a consequence? That's not right," he added, shaking his head.

"Yes. William needs to learn that his behavior impacts others. Children will rise to the occasion, particularly once they realize that their way of doing things isn't getting them what they want. William is a social child. Peer pressure is powerful. You'd be amazed at what children can accomplish when they put their minds to something." Like many people, she believed that William could will himself to control his behavior. She didn't understand that ADHD was the culprit, not William. She didn't understand that in order to help him change, she had to change her teaching style.

I sat on the sidelines, watching Bill transform from his usual Norwegian spectator mode into his attorney mode. His entire persona changed. He developed a terse look on his face. His eyes became narrow and squinty as if he were looking into the sun. His forehead pinched together, forming deep crinkles in the middle. His mouth sat expressionless on his face, without a hint of kindness or understanding.

"Ms. Smith, let me ask you a question. Would you be all right if your salary was docked each time one of your colleagues at school made a mistake? Does that seem fair to you?" he questioned, leaning forward now, sitting on the edge of his seat.

As I turned to Ms. Smith, waiting for her response, I noticed a constellation of red blotches forming on her pale white neck. At that moment, as much as I disagreed with her position, I felt sorry for her. I knew what it was like to have angry parents after me.

"I'll have to give your question some thought. I've used this teaching model for the last eight years. I hesitate to change something that's been very successful. But I understand your concern. I want to talk with some of my colleagues. I'll get back with you next week. How does that sound?" she asked, glancing back and forth between us.

Bill sat back in his seat, arms still crossed, eyes still narrow, slowly disengaging from battle. "That's fine," he said. Without another word or glance in our direction, he stood up, pushed in his chair, and walked out of the classroom.

Bill could be gruff and opinionated, but he rarely lost his composure. When he did, it often took him days to recover. During cooldown periods, he was quiet and withdrawn. He glued broken toys back together in his workshop and organized the garage. I'd learned to give him space and to wait for his return.

"Thank you for considering our opinion," I said to Ms. Smith. My temples throbbed from the stress of the meeting. I quietly tucked my chair under the desk and left.

As we drove home in silence, a million questions ran through my head. Had we been crazed, bullying, over-protective parents with unreasonable expectations? Had we done the right thing confronting her? Should I have said more? Would she now target William even more?

I wanted to talk things over with Bill, but I knew

better than to try. It would be several days before we could have a rational conversation. I sat in the passenger's seat and stared out the window, biting my cuticles, catching glimpses of freshly carved jack-o'-lanterns as we drove four blocks home. I mulled over the meeting and our son's predicament. We could take William out of public school and enroll him in private school, but that would strain our finances and disconnect him from kids in the neighborhood. We could ride out the school year and continue to micromanage Ms. Smith from the sidelines, but that wasn't working. We could ask for William to be placed in a different first-grade class, but the principal rarely granted those requests. I could have put William in therapy with a behavioral specialist to help him learn to control his behavior, but I was already working on these strategies with him at home. Medication was an option too.

✳

My stomach lurched when I spotted Ms. Smith's email in my inbox. Each morning, when I opened my eyes, my mind flashed to different parts of the meeting: Ms. Smith's blotchy neck, Bill's clenched jaw, the hard scrape of Bill's chair against the wooden floor when he got up to leave. To calm myself, I closed my eyes and forced positive thoughts: William will find his way. Most kids with ADHD settle down by middle school.

Since our meeting, Bill and I had focused on our options. He wasn't hopeful that Ms. Smith would compromise. He wanted to tour private schools in Saint Paul and Minneapolis. Money would be tight, but he felt it was our responsibility to make it work.

When Bill was diagnosed with dyslexia in second grade, his parents made the switch to private school. He felt the smaller class size and close supervision helped keep him in line.

I wasn't so sure. Private schools didn't offer special education services, like small-group reading or writing help. On the contrary, they taught at an advanced pace. And their class sizes weren't as small as they were when Bill was in school.

I stretched out my legs on the couch by Ellie and positioned my laptop on a pillow. I held my breath and clicked on the email.

Ms. Smith had given our conversation considerable thought. She would modify her classroom management system. Instead of putting students' names on the chalkboard, she would tally warnings for students at her desk. Each student would have the opportunity to work toward the party each Friday afternoon.

Students could earn the ability to participate in Fun Friday having all of their work completed and turned in on time and by receiving two or fewer check marks during the week. Students who did not earn party participation would complete school work in the library.

Ms. Smith ended her email with a brief summary of William's behavior that week. He had needed several reminders because of distracting behaviors, particularly with another student who brought a Star Wars book to school. She could tell that William wanted "to do the right thing," but the book had been too tempting. Hopefully, he would make a better choice next week.

As I read Ms. Smith's email, I willed myself to focus on the positive. She had compromised. She was no longer writing children's names on the board. She had given each child the opportunity to earn party participation every Friday instead of working toward a monthly party. One child could no longer stand in the way of others participation. This would help protect William's social status. These changes were for the better.

Still, her email didn't sit well with me. Turning in schoolwork on time may be a reasonable goal for a super-mature, detail-oriented first grader, like my friend Nancy's son, Mark, but most kids that age need lots of reminders, don't they?

At work, I redirected kids all day long.

On my days off, after I walked William to school, I watched how carefully children unloaded their backpacks, placed their lunches in designated bins, hung up their coats, and lined their shoes by the door. I noticed their hefty, worn Harry Potter books too. Later, I learned from the school principal that William's cohort was one of the most advanced that had gone through this school.

At the time, the high concentration of brainiacs felt like a cruel joke. William was reading *The Enormous Potato* and *Danny and the Dinosaur Go to Camp*.

This school, located several blocks from the

University of Minnesota, drew a high concentration of professors and other professionals. But despite my professional status, I felt like an outsider. I wasn't from Minnesota, I worked outside of the home, unlike many mothers in the neighborhood, and my son wasn't keeping up in school. I overheard parents discussing after-school activities like Destination Imagination, a parent-led program that helps children develop creative and collaborative problem-solving skills. I thought about encouraging William to join, but the idea of adding anything to our schedule felt daunting.

Getting William through his homework was hard enough. Each night, he had to read for twenty minutes, review spelling words for the Friday test, and complete a sheet of math. I'd overhear other parents laugh about what a joke the homework was, but to us, it was no laughing matter. Night after night, William repeatedly misread and misspelled the same simple words; *at* was *ati*; *he* was *hat*. This by itself wasn't that big of a deal, but his relentless movement was. Usually, during our reading time, I sat flanked between Emma and William on the couch, *The Enormous Potato* in William's hands. The image of the giant potato would zoom to my right, the ceiling, and finally to the ground when it fell out of William's hands.

For the love of God, I thought. Why does our nightly reading have to be so difficult? The farmer in William's book and I had a lot in common. He couldn't singlehandedly wrench a gargantuan root vegetable from the ground, and I couldn't singlehandedly teach William to read.

But even though I knew William showed signs of learning disabilities, my denial colluded with his teacher's nonchalant attitude; sure, he was a little behind in reading, but children learn to read at different paces. She thought we should wait until at least second grade to pursue private tutoring. Deep down, I knew waiting any longer was a bad idea.

But William's academic lag wasn't the only problem. Even after our immense effort to complete his homework, he rarely remembered to turn it in. His teacher believed that, eventually, William would grow so tired of the consequences that he would prioritize turning in his work.

I'd fire off an email to her about ADHD and memory challenges, and she'd fire one back about the need to believe in him, not cater to his weaknesses. This lack of understanding about ADHD and how it played out in William's life intensified my panic and obsession with his homework. If I couldn't control his brain, I could control his homework.

I developed systems to get the job done. I labeled William's homework folder in bold ink: "TURN IN" on one side for completed work and "STILL WORKING ON" on the other side.

This type of support often helps with ADHD kids, but it usually takes a teacher's involvement. That school year, most days, William's completed homework came home on the TURN IN side. This stunk, but William's inability to focus wore me down the most.

"Time to get ready for bed," I'd say as William sat in the living room cradling his huge Greek mythology book. At four, Emma rarely left my side. Once she knew it was bedtime, she'd climb the stairs quickly. The sooner she finished her bedtime routine, the sooner I would lie by her in her room.

"Come on," I'd prod William, sliding the book out of his hands, then searching for eye contact. Once our eyes met, he'd smile, surprised to see me.

"William, you need to get ready for bed. Go brush your teeth," I'd say. I could hear Emma turning off the water at the bathroom sink.

"Okay, Mommy," William would answer, meandering slowly down the hall and brushing one hand along the wall.

When I remembered to check on William, I'd find him perched on the stool in front of the sink, staring at himself in the mirror out of the corner of his eye, a slight grin on his rounded face. When I had the patience, I'd watch from the hallway, curious about what he'd been doing.

"Donatello, you dirty rat. You've caused me enough trouble. *Now*, you face Shredder," he'd threaten, mimicking Raphael in *Teenage Mutant Nin a Turtles*.

Then, out of nowhere, his facial expression would change, as if he had suddenly challenged himself to a staring contest.

"William, what are you doing? *Brush your teeth*," I'd demand, tapping him on the shoulder, leading him down from the stool by the hand.

"Mommy, did you know that Donatello likes that song *Frère Jacques, Frère Jacques, dormez-vous, dormez-vous?* Isn't that about going to sleep?" he'd ask with a smile, swaying from side to side as I held his chin in place and brushed his teeth.

At the office, I'd noticed similar stares in other ADHD children. This explained why researchers referred to the predominately inattentive type of ADHD as the Sluggish Cognitive Tempo type. These children are the daydreamers who were easily confused and mentally preoccupied.

The hyperactive-impulsive subtype of ADHD includes the children who need more movement than the rest of us. These kids barrel past me when I greet them in the waiting room, brushing their hands along the walls all the way to my office.

Kids who have symptoms from both groups, like William, met criteria for ADHD, combined type. He hadn't received this diagnosis yet, but I expected it in the future. If William had ADHD, combined type, it was no wonder he couldn't meet Ms. Smith's expectations. Getting through the week with no more than two warnings seemed nearly impossible for most first graders. For William, the chances were comparable to finding an oyster on a beachside stroll with a shiny pearl tucked inside.

I pushed my laptop onto the couch and pulled Ellie into my lap. I knew what Bill's reaction would be, but I wasn't ready to consider private school. I still held out hope that Ms. Smith would have an aha moment and change her approach.

At the beginning of the school year, when her frustration toward William became apparent, I sent her articles about the overlap between ADHD and sensory processing disorder. Researchers have found that children with ADHD can't block out sensory stimulation in their environments like their peers. Instead, kids with ADHD get so distracted and bothered by sensory input, like subtle background noise, that it brings them off task.

This described William perfectly. Daily, he asked Bill or me to "squeeze" him or lie on him in the evening in an attempt to settle his keyed-up sensory system. We did our best to accommodate him at home. Sadly, our crappy insurance (I will not mention names) would not cover occupational therapy services.

I didn't expect Ms. Smith to act as an occupational therapist, but if she had allowed William to chew gum or use a wiggle seat, maybe he wouldn't have left his seat so often. The gum may have ended up in someone's hair, but then we could have ruled out gum as a practical option for addressing William's sensory needs.

Ms. Smith probably would have felt better about herself if she'd flexed more too. Blocking William from Fun Friday, week after week, must have whittled away at her conscience. At work, I feel terrible when I send a child home, even if they've stepped way over the line (think choking my doctoral intern with a Harry Potter cape and snapping my glasses in half). Usually, I can pinpoint the moment I pushed too hard, stuck on my own agenda.

By the middle of first grade, even with Ms. Smith's modified classroom rules and our homemade rendition of occupational therapy, things had not improved for William in school. I considered bringing him to a child psychologist, but I felt I should have the wisdom and stamina to address William's problems myself. Besides, what would a child psychologist tell me that I didn't already know? I'd read stacks of books about ADHD. I knew way more about ADHD than his pediatrician and teachers. Why waste our time and money?

Looking back, I can tell you exactly why we should have sought professional help.

I needed the support.

Badly.

A good child psychologist would have kindly taken a chisel and chipped away at my barriers. She would have forced me to look at my role in our hectic life: When did I plan to face my perfectionism head-on and tell it to take a flying leap? What responsibilities had I taken on that I could release?

Instead, I relied on friends. I had joined a book club (aka "wine club" by Bill), and I cardio-kicked with my "Y Ladies" on Saturday mornings in exercise class. But we rarely shared deeply about our troubles, at least back then. I went to the YMCA to get away from my problems.

I spoke with a few colleagues about William, which was comforting. They understood ADHD. They validated my efforts as a parent. They also made me laugh, especially when I told them about our creative attempts at feeding and occupational therapy. When they recommended that Bill and I consider putting William on medication, I listened. I had relationships with pediatric neurologists, psychiatrists, psychologists, social workers, and psychiatric nurse practitioners. I knew that medication was a standard ADHD treatment.

At work, I had observed countless children on and off ADHD medication. Some improved dramatically from the tiniest pinch. The thick fog that clouded their minds lifted. Suddenly, they could sit through meals, tie their shoes, write their names, and sound out unfamiliar words.

Medication didn't erase all evidence of ADHD—they were still fidgety and dreamy—but it dampened the symptoms.

Near the end of first grade, Bill and I consulted with William's pediatrician, Dr. Kindly, about medication. I didn't like it, but I knew I needed to face it. Waiting came with other consequences, like low self-confidence and worsening academics.

Dr. Kindly requested a copy of William's evaluation from Children's Hospital. He asked us to have William's kindergarten and first-grade teachers complete ADHD questionnaires too. Bill and I completed a parent version.

During the office visit, Dr. Kindly reviewed the results. All three questionnaires pointed to a diagnosis of ADHD, combined type. I wasn't surprised when Dr. Kindly recommended that we start William on Ritalin, a stimulant. Ritalin has been used to treat ADHD since the 1960s. All in all, the research I had read on the use of Ritalin in children concluded that if the medication helped control the ADHD symptoms, the benefits outweighed the risks.

While the media portrayed stimulants, like Ritalin, as a possible gateway drug to other substances, research in reputable scientific journals suggested that this was false. Specialists in ADHD, like Russel Barkley, found that stimulant treatment in childhood was unrelated to drug use in adolescence. "It's not the Ritalin, it's the ADHD that might lead to smoking or substance abuse," agreed William Pelham Jr., professor of psychology, psychiatry, and pediatrics at State University of New York–Buffalo. In his research, he and his colleagues found that stimulant use might even protect against later drug abuse and alcoholism in children with ADHD by relieving the problems that often lead to substance abuse. It also showed that the earlier the stimulants are introduced, the lower the potential for substance abuse later.

Stimulant medications work by increasing dopamine and norepinephrine neurotransmitters, which are deficient in individuals with ADHD. Dopamine is associated with improved mood and motivation, and norepinephrine is believed to increase arousal and alertness and enhance memory and attentional functioning. This helps explain why kids with ADHD struggle to regulate their emotions, self-motivate, focus, and retain certain kinds of information, like multiple-step directions.

It also helps explain why many kids with ADHD hyperfocus on video games, which provide constant visual, auditory, and tactile stimulation. In fact, some studies have even shown that medications, like Ritalin, can actually curb cravings for video game play in children with ADHD.

Two days after beginning Ritalin, William began to repetitively grab the back of his pants, inching them slightly to the left or right. The same sweats he'd called his "comfy cozies" no longer felt right. In an attempt to resolve the problem, I bought larger sweats.

Nothing helped. No matter how many times we reminded William to stop, the embarrassing grabbing and adjusting continued multiple times an hour. Ms. Smith noticed it too. Just like anyone else afflicted by a tic, he could only hold off the urge to adjust his pants for a short period of time before he needed to carry out the movement again.

When we notified his pediatrician, Dr. Kindly, he recommended that we stop the Ritalin altogether. Ms. Smith hadn't noticed a benefit anyway. The pants-adjusting disappeared as quickly as it developed.

Next, Dr. Kindly recommended Adderall, an amphetamine salt medication known to enhance attention and diminish hyperactivity. It had similar side effects to Ritalin, but Dr. Kindly noted that it generally triggered fewer tics.

Ms. Smith emailed me the first day he was on it, a Friday, my day off. She noticed a change from the minute he walked in her classroom that morning. She said the Adderall sliced William's restless energy level in half. Instead of walking around the room, he stood by his desk. Instead of taking his mechanical pencil apart and rolling the tiny lead inserts across his desk, he completed a page of math.

This was the first time we'd received positive feedback from Ms. Smith. As I took in the moment, I leaned back in my leather armchair in the living room and squeezed a throw pillow to my chest. Would Adderall turn William's life around? Maybe he could stay at the neighborhood elementary school after all.

✻

"Mom, I'm sitting still, but my heart feels like it's exercising," William announced from the back seat of the car a week later, on our drive home from his school.

"Really?" I asked, faking calm.

"Yeah, I don't feel good."

I knew the most common adverse cardiovascular effects from Adderall were elevated blood pressure and heart rate (tachycardia). In rare cases, Adderall had been associated with heart attacks and even deaths in children. Most of these children had medical conditions that contributed to their outcomes, but I couldn't take any risks.

I drove directly to Dr. Kindly's office. He stopped the medication immediately. He reassured William that Adderall could cause his heart to beat faster or slower at times. Then, he referred William to a cardiologist. This doctor felt that Adderall was likely a safe medication to treat his ADHD symptoms since no one on either side of the family had heart-related problems.

For extra precaution, he wanted William to wear a Holter monitor for five days, a small machine that recorded his heart rhythm. The doctor and nurse taped small, round electrodes on William's bare chest and clipped the machine to his pocket. William was to push an alert button if he felt anything like he had in the car.

He left excited about the new game.

At the follow-up appointment, the doctor shared that the results were normal. His heart was healthy and strong. William could go back on the Adderall any time. We just needed to watch his salt intake. Too much salt could intensify side effects, like arrhythmia. Even though we had been given the go-ahead from his doctors, restarting the medication was hard. Who knows if this was related to negative press about Adderall or William's history of bad side-effects, but at the time, I didn't feel we had another option.

Not So Fun Friday

My heels clicked against the dated linoleum floors as I

zipped down the hallway toward William's classroom. I heard a collective burst of laughter and smiled reflexively. I loved being around children, especially when I wasn't in charge.

It was Friday, about a month after our meeting with Ms. Smith. I had arrived a few minutes early to pick William up from school. I hoped to surprise him. My last client had called in sick, which had been surreal. This family never canceled.

Bill was on his way to pick up Emma from day care. I envisioned the four of us ordering pizza and watching *Toy Story* in the living room in our flannel pajamas.

When another burst of laughter resonated from Ms. Smith's classroom, I slowed my pace. Had I forgotten something? Was it a special occasion?

Ohhh shit. Now I remember. How could I forget Fun Friday? We no longer received phone calls and emails of William's misdoings, but Fun Friday was still out of his reach.

I distracted myself by musing over children's self-portraits that hung on the walls outside of their classrooms. Some kids painted themselves in bold colors with sharp, chiseled features. Others drew with rounded strokes in soft pastels. William had drawn a thick haystack of blond hair on his head, big round circles for eyes, blue for shading, and a triangle nose with two dots for nostrils. His red, U-shaped mouth spread nearly ear to ear, which made me smile. Their artwork brought me comfort and perspective. Everyone's portrait was worthy; not just the portraits of the rule-followers who made it to Fun Friday. I could hear my mother. "Kath, being perfect is boring as hell. Color outside of the lines. Don't try to be like everyone else." I tried to keep this advice in mind while raising William.

When I arrived at Ms. Smith's brightly lit classroom, I spotted small groups of children huddled on the floor around board games and *Yu-Gi-Oh!* cards. A foursome of girls played jacks in one corner. Some kids glanced up at me and leaned into their friends, exchanging whispers: "It's William's mom," I heard one say.

I scanned the room for William's wavy blond hair. Ms. Smith sat at her desk, pen in hand, mulling over a stack of paperwork.

"William?" I mouthed to Ms. Smith when our eyes met.

She smiled quickly, pointed next door toward the library, and resumed working. My dream of a carefree evening fizzled. I stood in place, my heart thumping in my chest as I contemplated my next move. Should I approach her and ask what happened?

Nope, not now, I decided. I was in no shape for a rational discussion.

I spotted William from behind. He had laid his head on the table and cradled it in his arms. Two other boys at the table stared at their hands with blank expressions. I waved hello but got no response.

"Hi, buddy," I said, pulling up a child-sized chair to the table and forcing a smile.

When William glanced up at me, the lack of contrast between his blond hair and pale face struck me. Most nights, I'd awaken to William by my bed around midnight asking me if I would lie by him. It took another hour before his breathing slowed and I could sneak out of his room. The combination of lack of sleep, a nearly nonexistent appetite, and rough school days had taken a serious toll on him. Everything about first grade was too hard: sitting, listening, reading, writing, Fun Friday.

It was clear to me then that William's insomnia and minuscule appetite from Adderall outweighed the benefits. I saw no reason to continue him on it.

"Let's do something fun tonight," I said, patting him on the back, fighting the lump in my throat.

A weak smile grew across William's face as he sat up.

Let it go, I thought.

I pushed against my instincts to lash out at Ms. Smith or wallow in sadness for my son. I needed to show William that Fun Friday didn't rule us.

"Let's have our own party. You can get whatever you want at Speedy Market," I said with a smile as I gripped William's warm hand.

"Really?" he asked, confused.

"Yep."

When we pulled up at Speedy, William sprang from the car and hustled in before me. He picked out Ben and Jerry's cookie dough ice cream and his favorite

Irish white cheddar. I grabbed a frozen pizza, two apple fritters, and dark chocolate. That would cover Bill and Emma too.

That night, after William fell asleep, I scoured literature about ADHD and learning disabilities.

"Hon, go to bed," Bill said, nudging me to turn out the light. "You're going to exhaust yourself. You know how you get when you're too tired. You're a big crybaby," he teased, faking a sob into his pillow.

"Hush," I said, giving him a quick jab in the side, "I'm reading about tutoring for William. Your parents said you had tutoring as a kid."

"What do they know?" Bill answered sheepishly.

I knew that if I could help William learn to read and write, ADHD would be less of a burden. On the drive home, William explained that one reason he wandered around the classroom was that he didn't understand his work. I knew that the other boys in the library had similar struggles. I'd seen samples of their writing on the walls. Like William's, their print was big, with backward letters and multiple eraser marks.

Research continuously pointed me in the direction of Orton-Gillingham, an approach to reading and writing that combines visual, auditory, kinesthetic, and tactile components of learning to strengthen associations and memory. In graduate school, I learned that these multisensory strategies create new neuronal pathways for dyslexic children. I evaluated children for dyslexia at the office too. William was technically too young for the diagnosis, but more support could only help. During tutoring sessions, children formed letters with their bodies and drew letters in different media, like sand and shaving cream. That sounded perfect for William.

The next morning, I contacted Orton-Gillingham of Minnesota and found a listing of tutors in our area. After speaking with a handful on the phone, William and I set out to meet our top three. I wanted someone in Saint Paul who loved kids with high energy and could reel him in.

"We've got to go, William," I said, helping him slip into Velcro tennis shoes. He wasn't ready for ties.

"Don't go, Mommy," Emma said, climbing onto my back, tears in her eyes, as I tucked the tutors' names and addresses in my purse.

"You get to stay with Daddy," I said, smiling up at Bill as he cracked a smile back at me. He was well aware of his secondary status. "You and Daddy are going to get lemon cake at Starbucks, remember?"

"No," she retorted, flopping to the floor.

"Bye, Emma," William said, reaching down for a hug. Bill and I both blocked him and shook our heads no as William and I slipped out the back door.

"Remember what happened the last time you hugged Emma when she was mad," I said as we headed to the garage.

William opened his mouth wide and chomped down hard like a snapping turtle, reenacting the infamous event. "She bit me on the nipple."

PART FOUR:
An Upswing

Ms. Margaret

As William and I drove to the third tutor's house, my hopes rose. Maybe Ms. Margaret would be the one. She had to be better than the other two. The first woman we met had a sweet smile, but during the twenty minutes we chatted in her living room, she only took fleeting glances at William. The second woman didn't smile.

Something about my conversation with Ms. Margaret earlier that week felt right. Her matter-of-fact tone of voice soothed me. I liked her honesty too. After twenty years of teaching in a private school, she quit. She wanted to learn how to reach the kids who didn't catch on like the others. She completed two years of training in Orton-Gillingham and set up shop at home. She had been a private tutor for six years.

Before Ms. Margaret and I got off the phone, I added one last comment. I wanted her to have the full picture.

Why waste our time? "William was tested last school year at Children's Hospital. He has ADHD," I said, pacing in circles around the living room.

"Thanks for letting me know," she said as if I'd mentioned something as mundane as William's height and weight. "I look forward to meeting with you both."

"Me too," I said before I hung up.

I had explained the plan to William, and he hadn't protested. It wasn't his style to ask questions about appointments unless injury was involved, like a shot. He was more interested in battleships and geography. He couldn't read the words, but somehow, he managed to glean oodles of information from picture books.

Ms. Margaret's street was lined with small, cream-colored, Tudor-style stucco homes, each a slight variation of the next. Even though it was late October and winter was approaching, her yard was full of life. Her plush green grass, shapely bushes, and potted flowers stood tall and alert. As we climbed the front steps, I spotted signs of a gardener tucked in the corner on the front porch—potting soil, a trowel, and floral gloves. Her door was ajar, and a wooden sign on the porch in the shape of a teddy bear read, "Please Come In."

I rang the bell and waited, William's small, warm hand in mine. Ms. Margaret greeted us at the door and invited us in. She appeared to be in her early sixties. She wore simple clothing and wire-rim glasses. Her hair was pulled back into a tight bun.

Maybe it was her perfect posture, steel-blue eyes,

solid handshake, or even the rosary around her neck. Who knows? But from the minute I lay eyes on her, I liked her.

As we moved into the tiny entryway, religious relics revealed themselves from all directions. There were statues of saints and crucifixes on every wall. As I scanned her home, I was surprised by her religious interest. You don't meet people every day who go all-out and embrace God the way she did.

But my guard was up. I didn't want to put William into the hands of a religious fanatic. I was raised by a hippie mother who had steered me away from anything conventional. "Think for yourself," she preached whenever she sensed I was joining the masses.

Ms. Margaret shook William's hand and invited him into the tutoring room, sparsely decorated with a small white desk, two wooden chairs, a tall white cabinet, and a large, glossy poster of Catholic saints.

"Come on in, William. You can sit right here," she said, pointing to the chair across from her at the desk. I stood in the doorway, peering in.

She placed a small, black velvet bag on the table and smiled at William.

"Put your hand inside. See if you can guess what it is."

William smiled playfully, intrigued by the game. He stuck his hand inside the bag and rolled the object around, giving it a thorough feel. "It's an orange," he said, self-assured.

"You're right, William!" she exclaimed, clapping her

hands together. "You're good at this," she said, eyeing him with admiration as if he'd just added three-digit numbers in his head. "You know what *that means*?" she asked, a big smile on her face.

"What?" William asked, hopping out of his seat.

"It means that you can learn to read and write," she said, her eyes wide. "You know why?" she asked.

"Why?" he asked with a smile, his feet thumping against her desk.

"Because I teach kids to read and write with their senses."

Ms. Anderson

It was early June and children were scattered throughout the playground screeching with delight as I approached the school. I walked up the cinder block front steps, checked in with the receptionist, and sat down in a hard-bottomed chair, mentally reviewing the points I wanted to make in my head. Shortly afterward, Ms. Jacobs opened her office door and invited me in. From her placid smile and distant gaze, I wondered if retirement was on her mind.

"Hi, I'm not sure if you remember me. I'm William Quie's mother," I said, extending my hand with a shy smile.

"Yes, of course," she said, pulling out a chair for me,

sitting down on the other side of the circular wooden table. "How can I help?"

"Well, I know you just sent out a newsletter asking parents not to request teachers, but I can't stay silent. I'm concerned about my son. He's had a hard first-grade year."

I could feel my cheeks redden, something I'd grown accustomed to whenever I acknowledged William's troubles. His ADHD diagnosis was still new. In those early years, grief snuck up on me like a flat tire on a scenic Sunday drive. I could go from feeling carefree, enjoying the landscape of life, to deflated, stuck in a ditch on the side of the road.

I cleared my throat and continued. "When we met earlier in the year, I asked about moving William to a different classroom. I remember you saying it would be too disruptive. I didn't press because I wanted to believe things would improve. The sad part is that they didn't."

Hands clasped in her lap, Ms. Jacobs nodded at the right times, tracking my story. "Some years are more difficult than others," she said, holding the same equable smile.

"William went through a lot this year. He had to sit in the library every Friday afternoon doing work while his classmates partied next door. Ms. Smith is probably a good teacher, but she doesn't understand how to work with children with ADHD," I said, making sure to hold her gaze. My tendency was to avoid confrontation, not to make waves.

"Ms. Quie, *all* of my teachers are well trained," she

responded, sitting more upright in her chair, hands now tightly clasped in front of her on the desk.

"Ms. Jacobs, I'm not here to criticize your teachers. You run a great school. I just think some teachers are better with kids like William than others. I've heard from many parents that Ms. Anderson is great with active boys."

My main goal was to circumvent William's placement with a second-grade teacher, Ms. Jarvis, who had a reputation for cruelty. Not only did she sequester outliers, but she also berated them publicly. Each year, panicky parents strategized about how to keep their children out of her clutches. They wrote Ms. Jacobs letters, transferred their children to other schools, and prayed for a miracle.

Some parents were more stoic. They claimed that life is full of hills and valleys; if next year brought a valley, so be it. I had no time for passivity—not after what we'd been through.

"I understand what you'd like for William," Ms. Jacobs answered. "Parents get nervous about Ms. Jarvis, but she's an experienced second-grade teacher. Children learn a lot in her class."

"I'm sure Ms. Jarvis is good with most students. But if William is assigned to her class, we won't be sending him back to this school in the fall. I want him to stay at the neighborhood school, but I've heard too many stories about how frustrated she gets with kids like William."

Several months earlier, William had spent the day at a private school in Minneapolis, the only one we'd considered that was less than twenty grand a year. When I picked him up that afternoon, he sat in a chair outside of the office, leafing through a pamphlet about the school. He smiled and thanked the young woman who'd chaperoned him, and we headed out to the car, hand in hand. Once the car door slammed shut, William's disposition flipped.

"Mom, *please* don't send me to Jesus school. I promise I'll listen better next year."

"*Jesus school?* What do you mean?" I asked, surprised by his reaction. It was a Christian school, but it didn't have a reputation as being over-the-top, at least not from what I'd heard.

"They prayed *all the time*, Mom. Before lunch, at lunch, after lunch. They were nice, but they pray too much for me. I just don't want to go there," he said, tearing up and covering his face.

"Dad and I have to talk. We'll figure something out," I answered, disappointed. This school was supposed to be our backup plan if he got Ms. Jarvis.

"Mom, I just want to go to *my school* with my friends."

"We'll see," I said. This was not his decision to make. But Bill and I knew he would be miserable if he was placed with a punitive teacher like Ms. Jarvis.

※

After I made my final push for Ms. Anderson, I stood up and pushed in my seat. Ms. Jacobs walked to the door and shook my hand. "I'll consider your request, but I can't make any promises," she said.

"I understand. Thanks for your time."

As I left the building, I tried to shake off the tension from the meeting. My head pounded with each step I took down the front steps of the school. I slipped on my sunglasses and waited for the throbbing to subside as I watched a pack of children, maybe first graders, taking turns climbing a huge, knotty oak tree in the center of the playground. They nestled in the lower branches and swung their legs back and forth, squealing down at their friends with excitement.

I wished I could morph back to childhood, when life had been so simple. I hated being a pushy parent. Still, I cringed at the idea of William having a cruel teacher more than I cringed at my pushiness. As I walked home, I couldn't help but wonder if meeting with Ms. Jacobs had done him more harm than good. Why would she care if I pulled William from school? Her life would be simpler without both of us, I thought.

✳

Two weeks before school started, we received William's teacher assignment. My hands trembled as I ripped the letter open on the front stoop. I couldn't even wait to open it inside. So much was at stake.

At the top of the page, typed in black ink, read the following sentence:

William Quie has been assigned to Ms. Anderson for second grade.

I held the letter tightly to my chest and closed my eyes, taking in the moment. Our plea to avoid the dreaded teacher had been answered.

I ran inside and called Bill at work to share the news.

"Hey, hon, it's me. Guess what?" I asked, sitting cross-legged on the couch, squeezing a throw pillow in my lap.

"You won the lotto?" he teased.

"No, but it's *really* great news."

"We're going to Hawaii?"

"*No*, William got Ms. Anderson."

"*Thank God.* You big worrywart. You've been stressing all summer for nothing. I told you it would work out."

"I know. I can't stop smiling. She's supposed to be such a great teacher."

As much as I had longed for Ms. Anderson to become William's teacher, we'd never met. I'd only seen her passing in the hallways, leading a group of starstruck eight-year-olds to lunch, physical education, or art class. Each time, she'd made an impression on me. Her long brown hair was often windblown, her clogs scuffed, her sweaters worn. Her teaching style resembled her appearance. Unlike Ms. Smith, who became red-faced when children fell behind in line, Ms. Anderson looked amused, swooping to the back of the line to pat stragglers with affection. When children guffawed at each other's jokes, she brought her finger to her lips, rose to her tiptoes, and snuck down the hall as if a sleeping baby were in a nearby classroom. Like a string of dominos, the children rose to their toes and followed suit.

My southern roots also drew me to Ms. Anderson. We had only been in Saint Paul for four years. People were polite, but they kept newcomers at arm's length. As a Houstonian, I was used to strangers who swapped smiles, advice, and pats. Once, at the grocery in Texas when I was in my twenties, an old woman took the avocados I'd carefully selected out of my cart and replaced them with firmer picks. "Those are overcooked, honey," she said, patting me on the back with a smile.

Ms. Anderson reminded me of my people. Entrusting her with William felt like he was spending the day with an affectionate, beloved aunt back home.

Before school started, I sent her an email about William. I explained that he had been diagnosed with ADHD in kindergarten. I told her about Ms. Margaret and how William's reading and writing had improved. I shared that we planned to let William play hockey in second grade, which hopefully would channel his energy well. She responded in brief, reassuring me that she would check in if necessary.

On the fourth day of school, the phone rang at midmorning. I dropped the sheets that I was yanking off our bed and ran downstairs to catch the call before it went to voice mail. Saint Anthony Park School appeared on the caller ID.

Shit. I forced myself to pick up.

"Hello, is this William's mom?"

"Yes, it is," I answered, heart pattering.

"This is Ms. Anderson, William's teacher."

"*Hi,*" I answered.

"I just wanted to let you know that the projector screen fell off the wall today and hit William on the head this morning. We've had the school nurse look at him. She's not concerned, but I thought you'd want to know. He's in my lap with an ice pack on his head. He's a real champ, didn't even cry. "

As I listened to Ms. Anderson, I basked in relief, an unthinkable reaction for most mothers who just received a call that their child had been walloped on the head by a dislodged projector screen.

"Thanks for calling. I really appreciate it. Let me know if anything changes. I'll be there this afternoon to pick him up," I said, rushing off the phone.

After I hung up, I sat down at the kitchen table and covered my pounding heart with my hands. I had assumed Ms. Anderson called to tell me that she was sorry, but William was too much of a handful. Once, at a Christmas party, a father had commented that if Ms. Anderson didn't make it into heaven after teaching his son, the rest of us were screwed. Given her saintly reputation, this phone call would have obliterated any shred of hope that William could make it in public school.

✳

By the middle of second grade, after six months of tutoring with Ms. Margaret, William's artwork changed. His dragons now had jagged tails and teeth. This improvement was not without hard work. William and Ms. Margaret spent hours during their tutoring sessions working on letter formation. William diligently copied words and sentences at home between tutoring sessions. Given his tendency to strangle his pencil with a mean grip, the same way I handle a golf club, Ms. Margaret insisted that he use rubber pencil grips, which made writing a lot less painful and exhausting.

One afternoon, as William stood at the kitchen table during a homework session, he clenched his teeth in displeasure.

"How do you make a *g* again?" he asked as I mopped the hardwood floors.

"Look at your instruction sheet. The arrows show you how to write each letter."

"But I can't make my *g* like Ms. Margaret's. It's too hard," he complained, suddenly on the verge of tears.

"She just wants you to try your best. Don't worry about doing it exactly like Ms. Margaret. She's been writing her *g*'s for years."

"I still can't do it, and she's going to make me do them over and over," he whined, angrily erasing the same lowercase *g* a third time.

Writing a *g* required every bit of concentration and effort he had. Tears followed many days. The combination of his difficulty sitting still, minuscule attention span, motor weaknesses, and tendency to reverse letters made the task feel impossible. Some days it was.

Weeks later, at conferences, Ms. Anderson smiled at Bill and me as we sat down across from her at the rectangular 1950s Formica table.

"Hello, sit down. Let's talk about your sweet guy," she said with a big smile, lightly adjusting her scarf, flipping her hair behind her shoulders.

From her body language alone, I could tell this was not going to be a conference from hell.

"William's having a good year. He's really taken off in reading, he's happy, he has friends. He and Sean are hysterical at recess. They're always making each other laugh, singing and making up songs."

Bill and I beamed as she listed off his strengths. I wasn't entirely surprised. I'd already seen evidence of Ms. Anderson's kindness toward William, something that went a long way with him. One night, as I scratched his back before bed, he'd mentioned that Ms. Anderson scratched his back in the library while he read his favorite book, *History of the World.* I wondered if she'd known that added sensory input helped quiet his mind and body.

Even though William was having a good year, his symptoms of ADHD hadn't lessened. He still couldn't follow directions with more than a single step. We had to repeat ourselves and stay by him to make sure things got done. He still fell out of his chair during dinner. Midconversation, he'd fidget too much in one direction and fall to the floor.

When I asked for Ms. Anderson's perspective about ADHD, she tried to put her observations into words.

"He's, he's . . . It's kind of hard to explain."

"Could you show me what he's like?" I asked.

Ms. Anderson rose from her desk, tossed a piece of pumpkin-colored paper on the floor, and went after it with excitement in her eyes, examining it closely.

Her demonstration helped and hurt. I teetered between relief and sadness. Seeing her mimic my son was reassuring. His behavior wasn't all in my head. Still, I had secretly hoped she would look at me with disbelief when I mentioned his diagnosis.

She crumpled the paper and brought it to an imaginary classmate, offering it up for discussion. Then, she circled the exterior of the room, paper in one hand, eyes searching for their next target.

Why'd She Have to Graffiti My Desk?

"Hi Katherine, it's Ms. Carter from Saint Anthony Park Elementary. Is this an okay time to talk?" Ms. Carter was William's third-grade teacher. I'd been impressed with her from the first day of school that fall. She stood at her classroom door and greeted each child with a hearty hello.

"Sure, I just need to let the kids know I have a phone call," I answered, motioning the kids upstairs.

"Is it Daddy?" Emma asked, yanking my hand. "Is he on his way home?"

"No, Emma, it's not Daddy. It's William's teacher. I'll be with you both in a few minutes," I answered, patting them each on the back.

"*Come on*, William. Mom said it's time for bed," Emma bossed as William tagged behind her up the staircase, sliding his Ewok action figure along the handrail.

I scouted out a private spot downstairs and decided on my favorite worn leather armchair in the living room.

"Hi, Ms. Carter. I'm back," I said, pulling my knees up tightly against my chest, catching a glimpse of our spindly young maple tree, nearly bare in early November.

"I'm sorry. I know this is a busy time of night. I just don't have the time to connect with parents during the day."

"Oh, that's fine," I answered. In my head, I knew I wasn't under attack. Mrs. Carter was a kind, thoughtful teacher.

"I was hoping you could give me some ideas about how to support William in school." Normally, this type of request would have been tough, but her sweet tone buffered my pain.

"Sure," I said. "I'm not sure how much I can help, but I'll try." Even though I was accustomed to teachers' requests for help with William, I felt shaken. Ms. Carter had a reputation for being an excellent teacher. She'd been teaching for twenty-plus years. What did I have to offer her on classroom management?

"*Great.* Can you tell me what you and Bill use to help

William stay focused at home? Do you use checklists or incentive charts? What helps?"

"We've tried about everything since his kindergarten years," I added, trying to think quickly. I knew a ton of strategies. I'd attended annual seminars on ADHD for the last five years, but when it came to William, anxiety clouded my thinking. "I've been using a visual schedule in the morning. If William can get everything done by seven thirty, he gets a dollar. I still have to remind him to check his list a few times, but it helps," I said, relieved I had something to offer.

"That's great. I'm *so glad* I called. The more consistent we can make home and school, the easier it will be for William," she said. "He's such a sweet kid. Smart as a whip too." Ms. Carter paused, as if she were about to say goodbye. Then she asked for my opinion about how to help William track instructions during independent work time. Since he loved to read, she wanted to use an incentive to help him in these areas.

I explained that William's math teacher put sticky notes with page numbers on his desk during independent work time to help him stay on track. He said it worked very well.

Ms. Carter thanked me again. I took in a deep breath and stretched out my legs on the ottoman as I absorbed her positive energy. Ms. Carter saw all of him. Not just the ADHD.

I lingered in the armchair before joining the kids upstairs. I pulled Ellie into my lap and gave her a squeeze. She stared up at me, her black eyes a few inches from mine.

"Isn't it great, Ellie? William has a good teacher this year," I said as she wagged her tiny tail.

✳

When I picked William up from school the next day, he didn't have his usual grin. He trudged toward the car and climbed in the back seat, pulling the door closed hard.

"What's up, buddy?" I asked, craning my head to catch a better glimpse of him before we headed home.

"Ms. Carter is embarrassing me in front of my friends. That's what's up. I don't want her to treat me different than the other kids," he said, arms crossed.

"How so? What's she doing to make you stand out?"

"She's giving me special time in a big reading chair for listening; she's got a picture of it taped on my desk. Then she sticks stars on it when I do my work," he added with a cringe, his hand against his forehead.

"Is that the part that's bothering you the most? The picture of the chair on your desk?"

"No, I hate all of it! I don't want extra reading time in a special chair. Nobody else gets it. I'm not a baby," he added, pressing his watery eyes.

"Buddy," I said, reaching for his arm. "I'm sure she won't make you sit in the chair if you don't want to."

"That's not even the worst part. She keeps *graffitiing*

my desk. She never used to be so dumb," he added, buckling his seat belt.

"What do you mean?" I asked, pushing back a grin at his choice of words.

"Ms. Carter keeps putting stickers with stupid notes on my desk," he said, pulling a Casper the Ghost comic book from the seat pocket in front of him.

"I don't get it, William. Doesn't your math teacher do the same thing?"

"He only does it once, at the beginning of math class. Ms. Carter is *always* putting notes on my desk. She's damaging my reputation."

You're in third grade, I thought as we drove the three blocks home in silence. What kind of a reputation could you possibly have? I knew I shouldn't make light of William's complaints. He rarely lost his cool. Somebody probably called him a baby in class, or worse.

But it was hard to be sympathetic. So often, my mind was caught up in finding a solution. How could I get William to tune into his world without drawing attention to his problems? Why did the math teacher's sticky-note method pass and Ms. Carter's flop?

When we pulled into the driveway, I looked back at William and tapped him on the knee. "I have to ask you something."

"What?" he asked, reaching for the door handle.

"Did the note work? Did you turn in your work today?"

William tilted his head and paused.

"Did it?"

"I turned it in, but it doesn't mean she's right," he said, pushing the door open, swinging his backpack over his shoulder.

"What if she made the notes smaller and only put one or two on your desk each day?" I added, catching up to him as we headed to the back door.

"I'll rip them off," he answered, heading up the stairs to his bedroom.

That evening, after the kids went to bed, I tiptoed downstairs, poured myself a full glass of merlot, dimmed the lights, and settled into my favorite armchair.

I scanned my go-to book: *Taking Charge of ADHD: The Complete Authoritative Guide for Parents* by Russell Barkley, PhD. All 328 pages fanned across my lap. The picture on the cover reminded me of William; a boy in a large field in mid-run, arms out to the sides, staring off into the distance.

I had a love-hate relationship with Barkley. He wore stuffy tweed blazers and rarely smiled in pictures. He also forecasted a grim outlook for adolescents with ADHD and college, that only 5 percent attend a four-year university. What did he really know about ADHD anyway? Sure, he'd researched the disorder for years, but had he lived it? Raised someone with it?

Still, I liked his general perspective: ADHD is a neurological disorder, not a personality flaw. ADHD is a diagnosis that impacts the whole family. Everyone has to make changes, not just the child or adolescent with ADHD.

That night, I reviewed Barkley's principles for raising your ADHD child:

—Act, Don't Yak!

—Make Thinking and Problem-Solving More Physical

—Practice Forgiveness

—Use Incentives before Punishment

—Externalize the Source of Motivation

Ms. Carter knew to pair verbal directions with something tangible, like a sticky note. She externalized William's reward (extra reading time) by taking a photograph of the classroom "throne" and placing stickers on it when he focused. She never held him in from recess for blurting or leaving his seat. From what I could tell, Ms. Carter's primary misstep was too much externalization. William didn't want rewards that made him stand out. I got it. He needed his privacy.

Before bed, I emailed Ms. Carter. We needed to come up with a new plan. William should be included in the decision-making. He didn't want to be singled out. The throne made him feel like an oddball.

✳

At the first third-grade teacher conference, Ms. Carter showed us a sample of William's writing.

"William's paragraph about your trip to the cabin is hilarious," she chuckled. "He has a way with words. But his spelling isn't at grade level, and he needs help organizing his thoughts."

Bill and I scanned the page. Cramped, misspelled words fell messily on top of one another. Each sentence rammed carelessly into the next.

Negative thoughts spewed from my mind, triggered by disappointment and fear of what was to come. How hard could it be to start a sentence with a capital letter and end it with a period? How could he memorize the dates of every battle in US history yet be incapable of putting a tiny dot at the end of his sentences? Why couldn't he learn basic punctuation? If somebody as perfect as Ms. Margaret couldn't teach him to write, who could?

My rational side understood that, with Ms. Margaret's support, William would likely finish high school. I also knew that about 70 percent of kids with ADHD have learning disabilities, and that learning disabilities in written expession are the most common within this population. William hadn't undergone testing to determine if he met diagnostic criteria for a learning disorder with impairment in written expression, otherwise known as dysgraphia, but he had many telltale symptoms: irregular, slow handwriting; a tendency to intermix and reverse upper- and lowercase letters, particularly *b*'s and *d*'s; a cramped pencil grip; difficulty spacing out words and letters on paper; and frequent erasing.

Still, my irrational side was less forgiving. It even guilted me into believing that neither William nor I had been trying hard enough. If we had, we wouldn't be in this situation. Since William wasn't capable of directing himself, the guilt homed in on me. It sounded something like this:

Hey you, crappy mother. If you had spent more time teaching William to write his *g*'s in kindergarten, he wouldn't be in this shitty situation. If you didn't work all the time, dictating reports for other people's kids, William would be way better off.

By now, I knew that guilt didn't play fair. But kicking it to the curb still wasn't easy. It took a lot of strength to remind myself that I wasn't lazy.

Bill didn't buy into guilt, either.

"My God, hon. You've busted your ass for William. If anyone's to blame, it's me. I'm the dyslexic."

Bill's comments helped me put things into perspective, especially when William complained. "Why do I have to keep seeing Ms. Margaret?" he asked, tipping his head backward. After two years of reading and writing support from Ms. Margaret, we had all hoped to take a break.

"You won't get tutored *forever*. Maybe you can stop when you're in your forties or fifties," I joked.

"I hate tutoring, Mom. Ms. Margaret makes me write the whole time. *It's torture!* None of my friends have to go to tutoring," he yelled, now on the verge of tears.

As a parent, I struggled to find the right balance

between compassion and moxie. I cared about William's feelings, but I knew I had to stay strong. We had to keep our eyes on his future. By now, we had the means to pay for private writing tutoring, and we would continue to do so until he was at or above grade level. Life was hard enough for him with ADHD. I wouldn't let him fall further behind by neglecting his academics. He was in good hands with Ms. Margaret.

We all were.

✳

A New Love

"It was like the guitar was a woman, hon. You should have seen him," Bill gushed, his eyes bright with excitement. "It was love at first sight."

I hadn't seen Bill this excited in ages. He and William, now eight, had stopped into a Guitar Center a few miles from the house. They were driving down Cleveland Avenue toward Target, and Led Zeppelin's "Stairway to Heaven" came on the radio. Like usual, they chatted about the music, especially the guitar solos. Bill had always been into rock and roll. He offered to take William into Guitar Center to check out the guitars for fun.

Bill told me that William was drawn to the gaudy guitars at first, like the Flying V and the heavy-metal ones. Then he spotted a black-and-white Stratocaster near the front of the store that was more his size. He took it off the stand, sat down on the floor, and moved his hands across the neck and body.

"Really?" I asked.

"Yep, *really.*"

Action figures and history were William's main interests, especially war strategy and weaponry. We didn't own guns or encourage his fanatical gun play, but they still found their way into our backyard, play hour, attic . . .

I've come to realize that part of William's fascination with guns was related to his tactile, kinesthetic learning style and insatiable appetite for knowledge. Each gun had a different weight, trigger system, historical context, and material.

That evening, when I'd asked William why he liked the Stratocaster at Guitar Center so much, he was vague.

"I just do. I like holding it," he said, clutching a stubby wooden handgun he'd made out of blocks.

I assumed he would lose interest in the guitar, but a month or so later, William's love affair hadn't waned. He'd even checked out books about Stratocasters at the library.

One night after dinner, William pressed us to take him to Guitar Center to take a peek. I wasn't the biggest fan of the dimly lit store where scruffy-faced men in black skinny jeans and rocker T-shirts tinkered with guitars and amplifiers. But I agreed to tag along.

William beelined it to the Stratocaster, pulled the

black strap over his head, and positioned the guitar against his slim hips, mirroring the rockers on the walls.

"Foxy lady," he sang, strumming the strings, swaying from side to side. He had fallen for Jimi Hendrix a few years earlier when Bill played his album on a family vacation.

Bill and I winked at each other and enjoyed the moment. I had to admit: the guitar looked good in his hands—way better than the toy pistol Bill bought him from Reeds Sporting Goods.

"Please, please . . ." William begged in the kitchen when we got home. Emma listened from the corner of the room with Ellie in her arms.

"It's not that simple, William," Bill explained. "It's a commitment."

I knew where Bill was going with this. I thought he was crazy at first, but the more I mulled it over, the more I agreed with his position. William should have to work for it.

"This isn't a seven-dollar action figure, William. It's a one-hundred-and-fifty-dollar guitar. We can't just take it back in a few months or give it away if you don't like it."

William slid a rubbery monster finger puppet on his pointer finger and waved him at Bill. "But I do liiike it," he said in his deep monster voice.

"Mr. Monster, do you want to know what needs to happen for you to get what you liiiike?" Bill asked.

"Whaaat?" William asked, all smiles.

"You have to practice guitar for forty minutes a day."

"Okaaay," he answered, having the monster shake his head yes.

"You have to take weekly guitar lessons too," Bill said.

"Okaaay."

"And you have to keep this whole thing up for two years."

William paused. Then he pulled Mr. Monster off his finger.

I'd expected him to require a year of practice for William. Two years seemed extreme.

"I have to play till I'm *eleven* even if I don't like it?"

"Yep."

"Why?" William asked.

"Because everybody I've talked to at work said the first year their kids played an instrument was tough. That's why I want you to play for at least two. By then, you'll know if you like guitar."

William walked Mr. Monster back to the junk drawer and closed it.

"So what do you think?" Bill asked, putting his hand out for a shake.

William shrugged. "I need to think about it."

Secretly, I'd hoped he'd go for it. I loved the idea of William playing an instrument. I'd read about all kinds of benefits children can get from learning an instrument, like improved memory, focus, perseverance, coordination, and reading and math skills.

Learning to play the piano had been worth my efforts as a child. After a few years, I knew a whole other language. I lost myself in Chopin waltzes, Scott Joplin ragtime, and Beethoven's "Moonlight Sonata." The structure and predictability of music calmed my nerves. Piano classes in college balanced my hectic pace.

Two weeks later, when Bill got home from work, William walked up to him and thrust out his hand. "I want to do it."

"Do what?" Bill asked with a smile.

"Play guitar," William announced.

"Well okay," Bill said, shaking William's small hand.

The next day, Bill purchased William's first guitar, the beloved black-and-white Stratocaster.

Unlike learning to read English, music came easily for William. Daily, he sat in our basement, his guitar across his lap, listening to Bill's CDs on a huge boom box. Jimi Hendrix's *Are You Experienced* was his favorite album. William plucked along with Jimi the best he could. When he flubbed a note, he'd press stop, rewind, and play, all with his big toe. Then he'd repeat it until he had the riff down.

Many days, getting him to practice and stay focused was brutal. He always wanted to put practice off "just a few more minutes." Over time, we learned that William did best when we broke practices into two shorter sessions: one before school and one after. That way, he didn't feel so overwhelmed.

Even so, unless I was downstairs in the basement working alongside William, he got sidetracked. The internal self-talk that most of us have—that voice that tells us to get started on something or to shift back to what we are working on—is very faint, if not nonexistent, in many children with ADHD. Since William struggled to filter out his surroundings, I tried to keep his practice space organized and clutter-free. That way, his action figures and books weren't lurking on every flat surface tempting him.

Since kids with ADHD struggle to sequence steps, given their distractibility and poor working memory, William benefited from step-by-step notes to help him stay on track during music practice. When he was little, the notes looked something like this:

—Turn on your practice timer for 20 minutes

—Review your lesson notes from last week

—Practice your C, D, and E chords

—Play "Imagine" by John Lennon three times

—Play "Sunshine of Your Love" two times

—Turn off the heater

—Turn off your amplifier

—Turn off the lights

It was most effective when William marked off each step as he went and then brought the list to us at the end of practice.

Our presence helped William get through practices too. Many evenings, Bill or I worked near William so one of us could help him shift back to his music. Psychologists refer to this approach as "scaffolding"—breaking up learning into chunks and then providing concrete structure and support with each chunk. Simply put, scaffolding is a temporary platform used to help children (or anyone, really) get to a higher level that they cannot reach alone.

William's promise to practice daily helped us all stay focused. If we didn't hold William to his deal, he'd be disappointed in himself. Plus, what's a few minutes of music practice a day? His action figures and history books could wait.

✳

The Saint Anthony Park Elementary School Talent Show marked the beginning of William's performance life. He had been playing for nearly a year by now. The talent show was held every spring at Murray Junior High School, just a few blocks from our house.

I'd gone to the show once to see a neighbor's child tap dance. I'd had no clue that it was such a major event in the neighborhood. The whole auditorium was packed. There was a wide range in talent. Some kids told knock-knock jokes, whereas others played piano concertos.

The night of the talent show, William strummed his guitar and sang "Sunshine of Your Love" by the British rock band Cream over and over in the basement. He and his instructor had chosen the song for the performance a few weeks earlier. The piece was interesting enough to hold William's attention but not too difficult. His teacher worked hard to find a delicate balance in music for William, who bored quickly with most beginner guitar pieces, like "Ode to Joy."

William had sung along to rock and roll since he

was little. He sang in the church choir, too, but he'd never sung a solo. We had no idea if he would choke and forget all the words on stage that night.

When William started guitar lessons, Bill had encouraged him to sing along whenever he practiced. Bill had heard that the learning curve was much easier for guitarists who buckled down and practiced playing and singing together from the very beginning as opposed to trying to incorporate singing later. William was game for the challenge. The guitarists he admired, like Jimi Hendrix, had mastered both.

That night, we hauled William's Stratocaster and amplifier to Murray a half hour before showtime. William wore his normal attire: a soft T-shirt and loose-fitting shorts. My stomach was in knots. I would never have chosen to perform in front of my neighborhood as a child. Bill wouldn't have, either. When William saw his buddies, he vanished into the crowd until the coordinator shuffled him backstage a few minutes before he went on. Bill and I sat quietly with Bill's family.

When the announcer called William's name, he pushed through the red curtains, stood center stage under the yellow spotlight, and faced the crowd with a smile. The announcer positioned the microphone and gave him a pat on the back for good luck.

Do your thing, William, I thought. When I heard his young, innocent voice, I couldn't help but smile.

The crowd cheered William on and chuckled at the sophisticated lyrics, clearly well beyond his years. I'll never forget my happiness for William that night. He was nine, but he had already been waiting so long for a moment like this.

After the show, a handful of parents approached me. I answered their questions about his music with pride. I scanned the auditorium for William, who was now surrounded by his friends. They shared active imaginations, theatrical skills, and kind hearts. Several would become musicians.

That evening, something changed for William and for our family. His passion for singing and playing guitar was no longer just our joy. From that night on, neighbors, often musicians, approached William in passing. He had become part of their world. They asked about his music, how his lessons were going, what inspired him. Sometimes, they invited him to play along with them.

Music wasn't William's only strength that school year. At conferences, his teacher looked at Bill and me questioningly when we asked if his writing was at fourth grade level.

"Yes, William's a good writer. He seems to enjoy creative writing," she said with a smile.

She laid an array of his work about butterflies, warriors, and rock and roll across her desk. William's handwriting and spelling weren't great, but his sentences now stretched beyond three or four words and conveyed greater meaning.

As Bill and I walked to our car after the conference, we scanned each other's faces. Not everything had been positive—she had described his ADHD symptoms as "pervasive"—but she thought his writing was like any other fourth grader.

We beamed with pride for William and Ms. Margaret, who had worked so hard to improve his writing skills. Fourth grade had not been an easy school year. We had continued trying medications for William, but nothing was a perfect fit. Stimulants, like Ritalin and Focalin, caused problems with his sleep and appetite. Non-stimulants, like Strattera, didn't work nearly as well. They also caused sleep problems, even though non-stimulants had fewer side effects than stimulants for many kids. But William's music, his close friends, and Ms. Margaret made life a whole lot easier for all of us.

Lonely Earth

In fifth grade, at school conferences, William's teacher handed us a folder of his poetry. She had compiled one for each of her students. On the cover, William had drawn a picture of a tree with red fruit, the trunk wide and tall, overpowering the circular branches. He had colored the background a deep blue and drawn spikes of color reaching for the sky.

At the top of the page, he had written "POENTRY" in large block letters. On the next page, "Lonely Earth" was typed in bold lettering. A bluish-gray photograph of the earth was pasted unevenly to the bottom to the page.

Lonely Earth
The orb of life drifting
A pale blue mass slowly rotating
Encircled by the never-ending black abyss
A light of hope in a realm of emptiness
Not alone but one of a kind it goes around like a top
that evaded gravity

As I scanned William's poem, I let the words simmer in my consciousness. I was struck by his choice of language, inaccessible to me at his age. I had been far more concrete at eleven. Truthfully, I still was. Poetry had never been my thing.

I smiled along as William's teacher flipped to other poems, yet my mind stayed back with "Lonely Earth." What did William's poem mean? Was it about him? Did ADHD cause *him* to feel alone in a realm of emptiness, spinning like a top that evaded gravity? Did William feel a light of hope about his own life? Did he appreciate being one of a kind? I had no idea. How could I?

I turned my questions on myself. How had his poem impacted me? That was easier. "Lonely Earth" gave *me* a light of hope. It reminded me to keep an optimistic mindset, especially about the things that don't come easily in life. William had made steady progress in writing. That's what was important. Was his spelling perfect? No. Did he feel proud of his poem? I think so. Was I proud? Yes.

Mornings

Back then, I needed a light of hope to get me through mornings. One morning, I peeked into Emma's bedroom. She was lying on her back in bed, tightly gripping her panda Pillow Pet, mouth wide open, sound asleep. She had been a grumpy riser but mellowed over the years. She no longer screamed with frustration when she couldn't get that little bump of hair to lie down perfectly.

"Hi, Ms. Emma," I said as I turned on her pink bedside lamp, sat down on the edge of her bed, and rubbed her back.

"Hi, Mommy," Emma said as she nuzzled up to me, head in my lap. Emma's dark hair was wildly tangled and matted against her face. Her floral bedding was twisted in every direction.

"Guess what? We're having biscuits for breakfast." I had learned to talk about food when I woke Emma; it comforted and distracted her from the realization that she would have to separate from me to go to school.

"Biscuits!" Emma exclaimed, sitting upright. "William, did you know we're having biscuits for breakfast?" she yelled to him next door.

I meandered down the hallway and turned on William's bedroom light. He was a hard sleeper, and his covers lay neatly over his body. Above his bed was a poster of Gandalf and Frodo from *The Lord of the Rings* standing arm in arm, surrounded by hand-sized colorful dragons and witches painted onto his light blue walls. Recently, William had added posters of John Lennon and Jimi Hendrix, reminding me of how quickly he was growing up.

"Hi, Mr. William. How's my sweet guy?" I asked, sitting down beside him, rubbing my hands through his short blondish-brown hair. William instinctively took his arm out from under the covers and laid it in my lap, palm up.

"Will you tickle my arm, Mom?"

"Sure, but only for a minute. I've got to get breakfast on the table and Emma on the bus by eight fifteen."

William craved physical touch. Even at eleven, he still climbed into my lap. In his preschool and early elementary school years, he'd stand with his back to Bill, arms held tightly up against his chest, asking for "more pressure." These behaviors, thought to be associated with immature nervous system development, are common in children with ADHD.

In the kitchen, I put Pillsbury biscuits on a cookie sheet, threw them in the oven, and looked for other breakfast options. I spotted a box of MorningStar tofu sausage patties in the freezer and grabbed a few for Emma.

As Emma entered the kitchen dressed in her Yinghua Academy uniform, she scanned the table, forehead pinched. "Mom, you forgot to put out our schedules."

"It's okay. Check in the stack of papers by the phone. I may have put them there."

She rummaged through the papers, and suddenly, relief showed on her face. She placed the schedules on the table, lined them up, and checked off completed tasks.

"Mommy, I made my bed, brushed my teeth, brushed my hair, and got dressed. And it's before seven thirty. Do I still get my dollar?"

"Yes Emma, you do." To earn allowance, the kids had to complete their morning routine by seven thirty. This had reduced my stress level exponentially since both children were financially motivated and worked to meet this deadline.

I originally developed a morning schedule for William. Then, I realized Emma needed one for different reasons. William struggled to get from A to B because of inattention. Emma struggled to get from A to B because of perfectionism and anxiety. Even with reminders, William still couldn't remember to make his bed, whereas Emma broke into tears if she couldn't make her bed perfectly.

I needed the schedule because, without it, I teetered between Ms. Brady on *Leave It to Beaver* and Ms. Costanza on *Seinfeld*. For a handful of days, I was calm and patient. Then, I ran out of steam. When William dawdled, I shrieked at both kids to grab whatever they needed and get out of the house. The schedule kept us all in line.

William entered the kitchen with a stack of books

piled high in his arms, nearly blocking his view, and sat down at his place at the breakfast table.

"Here's your schedule," Emma reminded him, pushing it across the table to him.

"What's that *smell*, Mom?" he asked, ignoring her comment, crinkling up his nose.

"It's Emma's sausage patties," I answered, faking relaxed. I knew certain smells took William over the edge.

"Mom, I can't sit at the table if those gross fake sausages are near me. I can't stand to smell or look at them. I think they have tapeworms or nuts in them."

William stood up and backed away from the table, arms up, as if the sausages might jump off the table and attack him.

"Emma, can you hurry up and eat your sausage?" I asked.

Emma poked the last patty with her fork and methodically chewed each bite while checking off items on William's list. She could tell by his damp, pressed hair that it had been brushed. She heard his electric toothbrush earlier, so she checked off "brush teeth." I had no idea how she knew he made his bed, but she checked this off too.

"William, did you turn out your light?" she asked. "It's almost seven thirty."

When she got no response, Emma quietly left the table and headed upstairs to check to see if William's light is turned off. "You didn't turn it off, but I'll do it!" she yelled from the top of the stairs.

If William heard her, he didn't show it.

"William, you can have a biscuit this morning, but I want you to eat something with protein too. What about an egg?" I asked.

I had brought William to see a naturopathic doctor a few weeks earlier, who recommended we increase his protein intake. I'd scheduled the appointment after reading a few research studies about the use of nontraditional supplements, like fish oil, to treat ADHD. Some researchers had found that omega-3 highly unsaturated fatty acids levels are lower in children with ADHD and learning disabilities, such as dyslexia. Supplementing the kids' diets with omega-3s, like essential fatty acids and docosahexaenoic acid, had produced clinically significant benefits. One theory was that fish oil reduced inflammation in the brain. Then again, a 2013 meta-analysis found less than a third of children with ADHD saw some improvement in symptoms with fish oil supplementation or limiting foods with artificial food coloring. Since we had started William on lemon-flavored fish oil, Bill and I had both noticed a slight improvement in his focus, especially the first few days he took it. That morning, the fish oil wasn't potent enough to break through William's force field.

"William, did you hear me? Do you want an egg?" I asked a second time.

William stared straight ahead, a fixed look on his face, as he chewed his biscuit.

I moved directly into his line of vision and repeated

the question. "Will! I'm talking to you! Do you want an egg?"

"*What?*" he asked, shaken.

"Good grief, I've been trying to ask you if you want an egg."

"Sorry. Not really, Mom."

"Then you can have peanut butter toast or a protein drink. Which will it be?"

William looked at me as if I'd given him the option of amputating his right or left leg.

"I guess I'll have an egg."

"Sunny-side up or scrambled?" Emma piped in.

"Sunny-side up," he answered with a shrug.

"I want one too, Mommy," Emma said.

I melted a dab of butter, cracked the egg, and dropped it carefully into the pan, relieved that the yolk remained intact. Food had to be perfect or William rejected it. I threw away perfectly good food in my attempts to get it right.

This drove my mother nuts. "Kath, he's not *King* William. He'll never eat normally if you keep catering to him. If he's *this picky*, he should make his own food," she'd say when she visited from Baltimore.

"It's not that easy," I'd answer, wishing she understood.

I would have thought I was nuts too. I'd never met a full-throttle picky eater until I had William. My sisters and I weren't picky. As kids, we preferred fruit salad and pasta at dinner to green beans and meat, but we could force down three bites of each to earn cookies-and-cream ice cream for dessert.

William was different. Finding the patience to deal with it day in and day out was beyond exhausting. Whenever I played hardball with him, I lost. Each morning was a scene, a flurry of eggs, sausage, and peanut butter toast. One morning, I made a perfect sunny-side up egg. William turned his plate with keen eyes, examining it. After a thorough inspection, he sat back in his chair and sighed. "Mom, this egg is making me feel un-comfortable."

"Just take a bite before it gets cold," I answered, willing myself to remain calm. How could an egg make him *uncomfortable?*

"The edge is brown. What is that?" he asked, pointing to the crispy rough edge of the egg.

"That's the good part. Just take a bite before it gets cold."

I stared down at the egg. Its yolk was golden and full, like a sunset at the lake. It jiggled just enough when I moved the plate, ready to ooze. Its crunchy edges were buttery and salty, just the way I liked it.

But none of this mattered. Even when I made a perfect egg, I couldn't feed my child, something all mothers are programmed to do.

I could give him a bowl of pasta and call it breakfast. I knew he'd eat that. But he needed vitamins. He had to start eating something with nutrients. I couldn't give up now.

William slowly cut a small bite of the egg with his fork and held it up in front of his mouth. His eyes watered. Then he gagged. I knew he couldn't take the final plunge.

"It's too runny, Mom. I want to, but I just can't do it."

If looking at a food sent shivers up my spine, I wouldn't have eaten it either.

Emma swooped in from the sidelines and scarfed it down.

I dropped a piece of wheat bread into the toaster and mixed the peanut butter to the right consistency. I spread it evenly over the toast and cut off the crust. "Here you go, mister. Put down the book and eat."

When I got no response, I took the book out of William's hands and placed it on the cushion in the bay window.

He barely made a dent in the toast.

But, he'd swallowed *something* with protein.

I'd accomplished my goal.

Little victories like this gave me a mini sense of control over the ADHD. It boosted my morale as a parent and my energy to face the next hurdle.

Simple Man

The audition had been Bill's idea. He'd grown up stuffing himself with fried cheese curds and Tom Thumb donuts at the Minnesota State Fair. Full-bellied, he'd found respite from the heat under large oak trees and marveled at the gutsy folks who took the stage for the talent show. Painfully shy himself, Bill fantasized about a life as a lead singer and guitarist in a band. He'd taken a few guitar lessons as a child, but his parents weren't musically inclined. Without pressure to practice, he'd lost interest quickly.

Bill's dream had resurfaced in William when he showed an interest in music. If he couldn't make it as a musician, maybe William could. For the talent show, Bill and William chose "Simple Man" by Lynyrd Skynyrd. William was impressed by Lynyrd's long blond rocker hair, smooth guitar licks, and soulful lyrics. Bill felt the country song about a mother's hopes for her son was perfect for the fair, especially for the farmers who drove from neighboring towns to show off their livestock.

William, now twelve, wore a pale-green guitar T-shirt, Teva sandals, and long, baggy plaid shorts. His bleach-blond hair was buzzed.

When it was time for us to leave the house, William zipped his acoustic-electric guitar into its case and slung it over his back, ready for the half-mile walk to the stage from our house. If he was nervous, it didn't show. An hour before the performance, he talked less, but that was the only change I'd detected in him.

When we arrived at the outdoor stage, I scanned the rows of benches and spotted Emma in between Grandma and Grandpa. Other family and friends were sprinkled throughout the crowd of several hundred. Emma smiled at me and pointed to her bag of Tom Thumb donuts. She was used to attending William's performances by now, mostly at blues bars around the Twin Cities.

Emma's love of food helped motivate her to join. She ordered the big, warm brownie with whipped cream when William played at Famous Dave's at Calhoun Square and got chicken wings on Tuesday "Open Jam" nights at Wilebski's Blues Saloon when William performed with the legendary blues artist Jimi "Prime Time" Smith.

But it wasn't all about the food for Emma. She showed a real interest in William's music. Many times, she'd nudge me with excitement when William was about to come on stage.

That night at the State Fair, the smell of grease and cotton candy permeated the air. When the announcer called William's name, he walked on stage and scanned the crowd with a smile. "I'm going to be singing 'Simple Man' for you today. I hope you like it," he said, adjusting the microphone and then sitting in the rickety metal chair.

The crowd grew silent as William strummed a few notes and tuned his guitar. William had flubbed the lyrics during practice that morning. What if he forgot the song? I thought as my heart pounded. His guitar was hooked up to giant speakers. Any tiny mistake would reverberate throughout the crowd.

Then I reminded myself that he was just a child. This performance wasn't about perfection, it was about having a good time.

When William began to sing, his voice resonated

strong and clear over the crowd, part child, part teen. Each word cascaded easily onto the next. He held the notes in places, emphasizing the importance of the lyrics.

I sat back and dropped my shoulders.

"He's my son," I said, nudging the stranger next to me, an elderly man who sat alone. I couldn't tell if he heard me, but he smiled back.

After William sang his last note, he left the stage quietly while the crowd hooted and hollered for him, cheering him on. Some people even gave him a standing ovation. Bill and I looked at each other and grinned. Emma scurried to congratulate William, who had now joined his friends.

The following week, I checked the mail daily for an envelope from State Fair judges. He hoped to make the cut, but the results took up a minuscule amount of space in his head. Maybe this was one of the blessings of ADHD: he got to stay in the moment.

The day the thick manila packet arrived in the mail, I couldn't wait to hand it to William as he walked up the front steps after school. When he ripped it open and pulled out the contents, a brief smile moved across his face. He had made it to the semifinals.

The next audition was similar to the first, except the crowd had doubled to five hundred people. Thirty preteens in Minnesota and neighboring towns had been chosen to compete for a spot at the Grandstand, a huge outdoor stadium where musical artists like Sheryl Crow, Santana, and even Lynyrd Skynyrd had performed.

Contestants and parents sized up the competition as we stood in line for a meeting to review audition rules. William kept to himself. The boy next to us was a saxophone player who'd impressed Bill at his first audition with his rendition of Adele's "Rolling in the Deep," one neither William nor I had witnessed. While his parents gloated about his wins and work ethic, the young man held his head high and nodded along.

The competition stiffened when the saxophone player changed into his performance gear. His suit and tie fit like Armani, his leather shoes glistened in the sunlight, and his dark hair was combed to the side just so. On stage, he pulled dark shades out of his pocket and slipped them on in sync with his background music. I scanned William in his faded Eric Clapton T-shirt. He'd only performed at school talent shows. This could be ugly. Secretly, I hoped the saxophone player would flub a note, but his performance was as polished as his outfit.

When it was William's turn, he walked to the familiar rickety metal chair, steadied himself, and planted his feet firmly to the ground. He scanned the audience with a smile and wrapped his red, green, and yellow Bob Marley guitar strap around his back, exhaling as he plugged in his acoustic-electric guitar and adjusted the microphone. The audience fell silent, all eyes on him.

Like the song, his performance was simple—at least he made it seem that way. William looked as though he were alone in the basement: his eyes were closed, face full of raw emotion, a hopefulness and sensitivity about life.

When William left the stage, he joined his friends in the crowd, who patted him on the back. We waited for at least a half hour while a handful of judges conferred in a tent in front of the stage. Then the announcer would call the first- and second-place winners to the stage. Only the first-place winner would move on to the Grandstand in front of ten thousand people.

"Our second-place winner is Michael Johnson! Come get your certificate. What a fine violinist you are. Everybody, please give Michael a hand!"

The audience cheered while Michael, who looked about nine, smiled shyly, staring mostly at his feet, took his certificate and scurried off stage.

"Are you ready to meet our finalist, who will complete at the Grandstand?" the announcer asked the crowd, waving a slip of paper in his hand. William sat still in his seat tucked between Bill and me, hanging on the announcer's every word.

"Our finalist for the preteen division is a talented young man from Saint Paul . . . who's got a knack for playing the guitar . . ."

All eyes turned to William.

"Come on up here, William Quie! Where are you?"

William moved through the crowd of people, climbed the stairs, and met the announcer at the side of the stage.

"So, William, this has got to be an exciting moment

for you," he said, patting him on the back. "I'm curious.
Who's your greatest influence, William? Who do you
want to share the credit with for your achievement?"

"Jimi Hendrix," William immediately answered with
a grin as if they were old friends.

＊

A few days later, on the evening of William's State Fair
performance, I pushed my stepmother, Kathy, through
the crowds. She had recently become wheelchair-bound
by a progressive nervous system disorder. She was thin-
ner than usual yet striking, as always, in her red silk
blouse, pressed white jeans, pearls, and Hermes scarf.

When I'd shared the news with Dad, I hadn't realized he and Kathy would purchase tickets and catch a
flight from Houston to Minneapolis two days later.

"*Tillie*, I wouldn't miss it for the *world*—not for the
world," Dad had said, calling me by my childhood name.
"I don't think *anyone* in our family has ever done something like this," he gushed. "We're coming."

Dad had a special connection with William. He
didn't have a son of his own, and William was his first
grandchild. They shared that same angular jawline and
middle name: Stewart. We all three did.

That evening, Dad and Kathy were all smiles. Bill
and I were a bundle of nerves as we ushered friends and
relatives to their saved seats.

I glanced over at William and his friends, all sixth

graders, a few rows behind us. William was eating his favorite State Fair food: cheese curds. I would never have guessed he was about to play for a crowd of fifteen thousand.

Minutes later, after the sun had disappeared, bright lights shone down on a boy—William—center stage.

I knew he would finish strong when I heard the confidence in his strumming. I held Bill's hand and listened to William's voice echoing throughout the stadium. I contemplated the lyrics, so apropos for the moment. "Simple Man" was written from the perspective of a mother talking to her young son about life. She encourages him and tells him that he has everything inside of him that he needs to be satisfied.

After the performance, as the judges deliberated, I hoped that William would place in the preteen division of the State Fair final competition. I knew he'd lost points in at least one key area—personability. The support staff had strongly encouraged the contestants to address the audience before they began performing, and he hadn't. But I still thought he had a chance at placing.

Twenty or so minutes later, the first-, second-, and third- place winners were announced. First place went to a dramatic show-tunes girl and previous State Fair winner. Earlier that morning during tech rehearsal, she had been reined in for hogging the stage with her pirouettes and split jumps. Second place went to a twelve-year-old girl who wrote and sang a warm song about her grandfather. I can't remember who placed third, but it wasn't William.

A few minutes later, William emerged from backstage. When he saw us, he gave a light smile, shrugged, and hugged me and his grandparents. Then he ran off with a pack of friends. He had a handful of rides tickets to use.

That night I realized that I cared way more about William placing in the competition than he did. It took me a few hours to shrug off his loss. From what I've witnessed in life, overidentifying with our kids is a pretty common parental misstep. We push our kids to do their best and sometimes forget what's most important. William had worked hard to prepare his music, and he had played his heart out. *That* was the important part. That's what I'd always told him.

An Alternative Approach

"Where are we going again, Mom?" William asked, buckling his seatbelt, then ripping open the granola bar I'd tossed into the back seat.

"You have an appointment with Dr. Johnson today, remember?" William had been on the stimulant Focalin for most of sixth grade. It quieted his mouth and allowed his mind to settle into subjects it otherwise resisted. A page of math no longer led to a half-hour negotiation. Music practice was less overwhelming.

But over time, like every other stimulant, Focalin

soured his mood. Smiling was an effort. Minor annoy-
ances triggered tears. I missed my buoyant kid.

"Are we going to have to play one of those horrible
games again?" William asked. "I don't know why he calls
them games, because they're no fun. You just sit there in
the dark doing nothing."

"Bud, the games are called biofeedback. They're
supposed to help you learn to control your brain better."

"I don't like the idea of anything controlling my
brain. I'm already in control of my brain," he retorted.

"So how was your day, anyway?" I asked, hoping to
shift the mood.

"Fine, I didn't get in trouble."

Lately, when I asked William about school, he answered like this. For him, it was all about not screwing up.
So many thoughts ran through my mind. I worried that as
parents, Bill and I put too much pressure on him to stay
out of trouble. I worried that he wasn't getting enough
support with his ADHD. I kept searching for that tidbit
of wisdom, that combination of treatment strategies, that
could help him. I knew that medication helped him focus,
but the side effects dampened his quality of life.

On this particular day, as I drove William to another biofeedback session, I rationalized that even if he
didn't improve with biofeedback, Dr. Johnson's firm understanding of ADHD and reflective nature made the
sessions worth our time—or, at least, mine. Dr. Johnson
was the first ADHD doctor we'd met who talked directly

to William about his diagnosis instead of trying to talk through me.

During our last session, he had explained that the purpose of the garden game was to teach William how to settle his mind and body. The sensor attached to William's finger read his state of arousal and heart rate. As we sat in the dark, we all stared at the black screen with vague outlines of images and scenery in the background.

"You see, the more focused and relaxed William becomes, the more his heart rate slows down, and the more parts of the garden will appear on the screen. First colors will appear, and then eventually we'll see animals."

William stared straight ahead at the screen along with the rest of us. One minute passed, then two, then three.

I can't take this anymore, I thought, squeezing my hands together and staring at the black, lifeless screen. For once, I was thankful for the steady thump of William's feet against the desk. Some input was better than nothing. Then, a touch of yellowish-green and white appeared on the edges of the screen. A lily? Waterfall? Grass?

"*Wow,* look at that," I said, as if William had done a backflip.

William sat stone-faced. Within seconds, the color disappeared, and we were left looking at a bleak screen again. "I'm bad at this," William said, slumping his shoulders.

"Well, you're not exactly good at it. Not yet, at least," Dr. Johnson said, as he turned on the lights. "But you'll get better with practice," he added, removing the monitor from his finger. "I wonder if this isn't your best time of day, William. What do you think?"

"I don't have a best or worst time of day," William answered, pushing his chair away from the computer, staring down at his feet.

"Well, it just seems like you're distracted today. What do you think?" Dr. Johnson asked.

"I'm just tired."

"Okay, I could be wrong. It's happened before. You know, I think I was wrong once in 1994—or maybe it was 1995."

William smiled quickly and resumed a frown.

Dr. Johnson shifted his attention to me. "Do you know when we're meeting next?"

"We don't have anything else scheduled. I'm not sure what to do," I answered, clasping my hands together, glancing at him and then at William.

Between sessions, I had gone back and forth about whether or not we should continue. William had only tried biofeedback four times, but each session he'd gotten so frustrated that he barely spoke on the drive home. Dr. Johnson had recommended that we purchase a program for our home computer to practice skills between sessions, but I hadn't followed through. I couldn't justify buying an expensive program when I could barely get William to cooperate in Dr. Johnson's office. Plus, research on its efficacy in ADHD children was mixed. One study I'd read showed that biofeedback helped some kids focus better if they practiced it daily, but the benefits didn't stick when they quit.

As we walked to the car, most of me knew we would never return. A little part of me, the pleaser part, wanted Dr. Johnson's approval. I sensed that he felt I should push William more. If we stuck with biofeedback, he would see that I was the kind of mother who put her foot down.

My rebellious, who-gives-a-shit part knew that I had nothing to prove to Dr. Johnson. I wasn't a slouch parent. I stood up for William in school, dealt with his insomnia and crappy diet the best I could, got him to drink fish oil, and gave him medication when nothing else helped.

Earlier that school year, Bill and I had also pressed to get William a 504 Accommodation Plan in school. The "504" refers to Section 504 of the Rehabilitation Act. It was developed to ensure that children with disabilities receive accommodations in school, like movement breaks, help with planning and organization, and extra time on tests. The 504 is designed to help all children and adolescents reach their potential.

William's fifth-grade teacher had recommended the 504, as well. We were in weekly contact all school year. She reminded William to turn in his work, notified me if he didn't, and documented William's ability to focus daily on a calendar to help us measure the effectiveness of his medication. When he couldn't tolerate the medication due to side effects, she tolerated more of his ADHD. She and William had a great relationship. But she wasn't moving on to middle school with him, which was just one year away. He would have a handful of teachers then.

Bill and I were both open to the 504. I had always assumed we would ask for one at some point in elementary school. But with Ms. Margaret, our help from home, and a few excellent teachers along the way, William had gotten by. In middle school, he would need a higher level of support. He would be juggling multiple classes, more homework, larger assignments. A 504 could have a major impact on William's success in middle school.

The principal jumped on board immediately. She had known William since kindergarten. She got it. But William's sixth-grade teacher wasn't convinced a 504 was necessary.

"What's the worst thing that can happen if he fails?" she had said, crossing her arms at the meeting. "He'll ultimately learn to take more responsibility for himself, which is necessary in middle school."

If life were only that simple, I thought. With most preteens, letting them fail would motivate them to get the job done better the next time. Kids with ADHD continue to make the same careless mistakes, day after day, consequences and all. The fact that William's teacher couldn't make this connection, even though she had kept the entire class in from recess one day because William had forgotten to write his name on his work, AGAIN, made it hard for me to be understanding. Research suggests that executive functioning in ADHD kids is delayed by about two to three years. That meant, that as a sixth grader,

William's ability to focus, plan, organize, and hold information in his short-term memory was like that of a third or fourth grader.

"If you don't think he should have a 502 or 405 or whatever you want to call it, then I want him to have an IED," Bill said, eyeing William's teacher from across the table.

I tried not to laugh. All I could think of was an IUD. Bill meant to say an IEP, shorthand for an Individualized Education Program. I loved this side of my husband. The side that didn't give a rip if he spit out the wrong acronym in a meeting.

The principal smiled at Bill and explained the difference between a 504 and IEP; a 504 provides students with accommodations in the classroom, while an IEP is more intensive and usually involves support from specialists. It requires documentation of measurable growth too.

"I want documentation of his growth," Bill said. "My son has driven every one of his teachers nuts at this school. I'd think you all would want documentation of his growth too."

That's when the principal stood up, walked to her desk, and grabbed the paperwork for a 504 plan. She explained that if the 504 wasn't sufficient, we could meet again to discuss an IEP. She asked each of us to make a list of the accommodations we felt William needed to thrive in school. Did he need extra time for homework and tests? A specific seat in the classroom to enhance attention? Movement breaks? Planning and organizational help? William's sixth-grade teacher nodded along without a word. She signed the paperwork a week later.

*

A few weeks later, William's elementary school held an election for school president—a sixth grader. I can't recall the details, but William decided to run. He loved participating in the Saint Anthony Park (SAP) carnivals, field days, and school plays. He had performed annually in the school talent show since third grade.

My memories of William's pre-election preparation are both blurry and clear. I remember Bill helping him choose a few childhood photographs to enlarge and hang throughout the school as part of his campaign. In one photo, William is wearing bright yellow Bob the Builder protective goggles that tightly hug his chubby cheeks. He's gripping a plastic chainsaw, a look of determination on his face. The slogan read something like, "If you vote for me, I'll get the job done."

I remember William walking in circles in the living room practicing his pre-election speech. Like usual, his movements were dizzying, but his decision to run for president and his willingness to practice stood out. This presidency thing mattered to him. It must have felt achievable too. If I had been sent to the principal's office, library, and hallway as many times as William, I would not have had the nerve to make a speech about why I deserved the nomination.

William's creative edge, strong language skills, and enthusiasm likely contributed to his presidential win that year. His campaign posters featured someone who lived in his imagination, who didn't take himself too seriously.

These qualities likely contributed to his presidential blind spots too. Kids scowled at him at lunch when their gritty pears weren't replaced by real desserts like he'd promised. He hadn't realized that the cafeteria ladies couldn't just snap their fingers and make the Child Nutrition Division of Minnesota provide cupcakes.

During William's term that year, Bill and I gave him many pep talks. He needed to stay strong, even when his good friends expressed grave disappointment in his leadership. He would have to remain polite, even when adults took over student-led meetings. He was a role model now. He couldn't mouth off if clueless fourth graders infringed on his playground territory.

William's presidency at SAP was a big deal. He learned that if he really wanted something and put in a ton of effort, he might get what he wished for. He also learned that he'd better follow through on his promises.

Skiing

A few weeks later, as Bill, Emma, and I chatted about our

plans on the drive to Afton, William stared out the windows, listening to his MP3 player.

"What's wrong with William?" I mouthed to Bill from the passenger seat.

"It's his meds," he answered quietly. "He's always like this when we give him his meds on the weekends."

Bill's comment took me by surprise. Even though I'm the psychologist who analyzes children for a living and Bill is the product developer who analyzes data in front of a computer, I got blindsided when it came to William, particularly about medication. At the time, I couldn't tell if my lack of insight was related to relentless denial that wouldn't take its claws out of me or if I was simply a slow learner when it came to my own children.

Now, I know it was denial. I had acknowledged William's diagnosis, but that was only the first step. To me, this first step seemed akin to that of an alcoholic who finally admits that she has a drinking problem. The parent of a child with ADHD and the alcoholic have each taken a big step when they recognize that a problem exists. But facing the complexities that come along with that problem is far more difficult.

Back then, my denial protected me from crappy feelings like guilt. If I had fully acknowledged how crappy William felt on his medication, I couldn't have encouraged him to take it. At the time, the medication was our best ally. He didn't feel great, but he got his work done and stayed out of trouble. Plus, I worried about his safety off the medication. It helped him stay tuned into the world when he needed to, like when he was crossing the street.

That morning at Afton, the ski rental shop was packed with children and parents bustling about, preparing for a day of fun. We stood quietly in line, all facing forward, winding slowly to the check-in counter. William and Emma were herded to a separate counter and asked to stand up tall against a measuring tape that snaked up the wall. William was sixty inches—a whole five feet tall—which brought a smile to my face. As a baby, he started out huge, over nine pounds. Gradually, he dwindled to the tenth percentile for height and weight. By fourth grade, Bill and I had made it our mission to counteract his tininess with protein shakes and threats that he would be the smallest child in his class if he didn't start eating more than bowtie pasta. Who knows what triggered the growth spurt, but it finally came in sixth grade.

"What size shoe do you wear?" asked the twenty-something woman as she attempted to fit William for gear. After an awkward silence, she scanned Bill's face and then mine for an answer.

"He wears a seven," Emma, now nine, piped up. When we adopted Emma, we had no idea how handy her keen memory for details would be for the family—especially for William. By the time she was two, she'd scramble to find his shoes and place them carefully at his feet before we left the house.

These lapses in William's memory concerned me, but that morning, I was more upset about his deadpan facial expression and zapped energy level. At twelve, he was going snowboarding for the first time in his life. The night before, when I reminded him of our plans, he looked up from his Revolutionary War book with a big grin. "Mom, I'm so excited that it feels like it's coming out of my fingertips and toes!"

After measuring William for a snowboard, a young man with long, sandy-brown dreadlocks placed a bright orange helmet on his head. "How does it feel? Too tight, too loose?" William's eyes came alive, focusing in on the man's face, teasing us into believing he could shake out of it. The brightness in his eyes faded quickly.

"It's okay," he mustered.

Emma turned to William, reached up to his helmet with her tiny hands, and rocked it back and forth. "It's too loose," she asserted, looking the man square in the eyes, as if she'd been working there for years.

Afterward, Emma and William sat side by side on a long bench, preparing for their initiation into snowboarding. Emma's legs dangled off the bench, while William's draped over each other, sticking out into the aisle, oblivious to traffic. Emma laced up her boots and readjusted her helmet. She pulled hard on the laces, tightened and looped them around the eyelets, then wrapped them around each calf, ending up with a sturdy, double-knotted bow.

William loosely held a long lace in each hand and attempted to tie his boots. His hands, now the same size as mine, clung awkwardly to the laces and bumped into each other clumsily. When I moved in to help, he yanked the laces out of my hands. "I can do it myself," he snapped.

As Bill and I watched him struggle, I remembered why lacing his shoes was hard. Like many children with ADHD, coordinating his movements to write his name, play catch, and ride a bike hadn't come easily.

Loose laces and all, we set out to find Aaron, their snowboarding instructor. He was waiting for us on the beginner's hill, clad in an oversized snowboarding jacket and loose-fitting jeans. He smiled, revealing perfectly aligned, sparkly white teeth that couldn't have been free from braces for long. We told him we would be skiing with friends, we could be reached on our cell phones, neither child had downhill skied or snowboarded, both could cross-country ski and ice-skate, and we'd see them at three.

As we walked away, I tried not to second-guess. Usually, I spoke with William's coaches about his diagnosis. That morning, I held back. I knew that the boundary between helping a preteen and micromanaging was hazy and slick. I didn't want to overstep. But keeping quiet felt like I was selling a used car without giving the new owner secrets to a smooth ride.

After outfitting the children in gear and sending them off for lessons, the thought of spending the day skiing down tiny mounds of man-made snow felt like way too much work. I didn't feel great about Emma, either. I had barely acknowledged her all morning. She seemed unfazed. She'd learned to use her sharp memory to capture our attention. "I know where they are!" she'd blurt out whenever something was out of place.

The fact that I hadn't been downhill skiing in eight years added to my sour mood. I felt frumpy and middle-aged next to the newly outfitted, stylish young skiers sporting Ray-Bans and plush, fitted outfits. My ancient red North Face parka was misshapen and homely after years of hanging in the basement closet. When I'd tried on my black ski pants, they wouldn't even button until I pulled them up high above my waist, which made them at least three inches too short. My heavy, dusty ski boots cut off the circulation in my calves and toes, causing them to throb in pain. As a finishing touch, my tinted goggles were gargantuan, giving me a beetle-like appearance. Bill's tight, mismatched outfit looked even worse. Normally, this would have sent me into a fit of laughter, but I had lost my sense of humor heading south on Highway 61 a few hours back.

"I shouldn't have given him his medicine at breakfast," I lamented as Bill and I shoved our duffel bags into tiny lockers before heading out on the slopes.

"Hon, I would have reminded you not to give it to him, but he's got to be able to listen to the instructor. He'll shake out of it by lunchtime. The meds hit him hard in the morning. In a few hours, he'll be smiling."

"It still makes me feel crappy when he's sitting there like a blob."

It had been years since we began treating William's ADHD with medication, but my grief at that moment felt as raw as it had in the very beginning. I couldn't get William's comment from the night before about excitement coming out of his fingertips and toes out of my mind. I couldn't stand the terrible bind we were in as a family. Bill didn't take it nearly as hard as I did.

"The sad part is that he has ADHD. *That's* the sad part. The fact that he's flat and quiet once in a while isn't so bad," Bill added, giving me a light pat on the knee. This pat was his code for, "We need to move on, hon. You're starting to spiral."

That morning, I had hesitated before dropping the medication into the tiny, delicate Chinese bowl at William's place at the table. It was originally intended for ginger shavings and garlic, not one milligram of Guanfacine. I'd begun using it to keep track of the medication, which otherwise found its way under the place mat or onto the floor. The delicate blue-and-white dish also lifted my spirits. Years earlier, my mother had sent it in a package labeled "for stir-fry."

The effects of Guanfacine on William were both blessing and curse. On this particular day, the medication would help him notice snowboarders in his peripheral vision, prepare to jump on and off the chairlift, and remember the eight dollars in his back pocket we gave him for lunch.

For the first few hours after William took Guanfacine, there was not a shred of excitement in his toned, prepubescent body. His blue eyes stared back at me blankly as if no one were home. When I saw William this way, my mouth, accustomed to shifting into a smile, sat taut on my face.

When I asked his sixth-grade teacher if William sat like a lifeless statue in class, the perplexed look on her face told me she wasn't acquainted with this side of him. Maybe he was bombarded with enough stimuli at school to keep the lull of Guanfacine at bay. Maybe his mind slowed down enough to focus on a single thought instead of bouncing between four or five competing ones.

When I asked William how he felt on medication, I got different answers.

"At lunch, I can usually give somebody a milker." A milker happens when someone laughs so hard that milk sprays out of their nose. "On my meds, I don't have anything to say."

Eduardo, Bill's coworker and friend, had set up a time for us to meet at lift number five. He gave Bill clear instructions as to how to identify his partner: "When you see someone the size of a ten-year-old boy wearing a bright red, *stunning* outfit, that's Javier. You can't miss him."

I enjoyed Eduardo, but our universes were miles apart. He spent weekends at art exhibits, fine restaurants, and bed and breakfasts, whereas we spent *ours* at soccer practices, music lessons, and the kitchen table, enduring turkey burgers and homework sessions. Eduardo's svelte physique reeked of a childless life. His dark, flawless skin was striking for someone in his midfifties. "I've spent enough dollars on Aveda products to pay for a trip to Rome!" he gushed when I complimented his complexion.

We rarely had a day without kids. I would have

preferred huddling up by the fire and clicking away on my laptop, but skiing was Bill's favorite sport. I snapped into my skis and set out toward lift number five. My arms shook as I pulled myself up a tiny mound of snow.

"I didn't wear enough layers. I have to go back to the car," I complained three minutes into our adventure. If I picked a fight, I could go back to the lodge and hide out. He'd have more fun without me, I rationalized.

"Okay, hon, let's go back. You've got to be comfortable."

From a distance, Eduardo looked statuesque in a tan-and-white plaid fitted jacket and white designer ski pants. Javier, all in red, came up to Eduardo's shoulders. They waved furiously with both hands when they spotted us. At that moment—bad mood, bad outfit, bad wife, bad mother, and all—I stopped resisting. I had never received a more enthusiastic greeting in my life. I smiled big and skied toward them, soaking up their excitement.

For the next four hours, we skied in a small pack from one end of Afton to the other. We raced across icy catwalks, through tunnels, and down moguls. I became attuned to my body, less caught up in my mind. I noticed the burn of my quads as I swerved back and forth across the snow. I felt my warm breath circulating beneath my scarf. I focused on making the next turn, not heady decisions like which class of medications we should try next on William. I no longer cared about my outdated clothing or longed for time alone.

I checked my watch. It was two thirty. I was stunned at how time had flown. After hugging our friends and waving them off, Bill and I skied to the beginner slope.

I scanned the area for an orange helmet, William, and a dark green jacket, Emma. I spotted them in the ski lift line with Aaron at the bottom of the hill. I breathed a sigh of relief.

"Mommy!" Emma yelled. "Can I show you how I can snowboard?"

"Sure," I answered, moving in for a hug.

William was more subdued.

"How're you doing, William? Did you have fun?" I asked as we squeezed together in the lift line.

"It was fun, but I fell a lot."

William was ambivalent about more skiing but decided to go on one more run. His snow pants were soaked and his face was drawn. We split off in pairs—me with Emma, Bill with William—on the two-seated ski lift.

When Emma and I reached the top of the hill, she put her arms out to the side like a bird preparing for flight. She glided gracefully to a quiet spot, her front foot firmly planted on the board and back foot resting loosely behind it, and buckled her back foot in place.

"See you at the bottom, Mom," she said, pushing off and glancing up at me one last time. She maneuvered back and forth with her knees slightly bent and her face and shoulders downhill, as if she were listening to Aaron's voice talking her through each step.

William hopped off the ski lift but lost his balance

and crashed forward, hitting the ground with a thud. As I watched on, Bill skied to his side to lend a hand.

William pulled himself up into a seated position, buckled his back boot into the snowboard, and headed down the mountain without a word. He glided smoothly to the right, free and unencumbered, and fell forward on his hands and knees. He rolled onto his back and lay there.

"I've fallen at least one hundred times today," he announced, arms and legs out to his sides.

"Buddy, it's normal to fall. Everybody says snowboarding's hard to learn. You'll get it," Bill encouraged.

Emma waited for us at the bottom of the hill. "Are you okayyy, William?" she yelled.

"Leave me alone, Emma," he said when she repeated the question to his face at the bottom of the hill.

The drive home was quiet. We were all caught up in a new dilemma. For better or for worse, we minimized Emma's accomplishment to cushion the blow for William.

Later, as I lay with William, helping him fall asleep, he filled me in on the details.

"After I made the same mistake like fifty times, Aaron covered his eyes and stood there. He showed me how to turn over and over, but I kept doing it wrong. Finally, I got it. But then I couldn't show you guys."

"It doesn't matter, William," I said, rubbing his back, but my words fell flat. It mattered to him.

Behind closed doors, Bill and I schemed up a plan. He would take William for solo snowboarding lessons before our next family outing. More practice would make it more fun for all of us the next time we ventured out. Emma loved skiing with him. If she stayed at the top and he continued to flounder, she'd move into care-taking mode and he'd reject her. Neither option seemed as fun as having her big brother snowboard alongside her. The burden that she carried stood out more on days like these. I knew she was tough, but I also knew that life could be a whole lot easier for all of us if we could figure out how to manage ADHD better.

Dr. Michaels

The hood of William's black puffer coat covered his dark blue eyes, making it impossible to read his expression. Since his pediatrician had discontinued the Guanfacine, his mood had brightened slightly.

"What's wrong? Are you nervous?" I asked, turning to glace at William in the back seat. Bill and I were picking him up for school to take him to see Dr. Michaels, a child psychiatrist.

"No," he answered, still fixed on the bleak outdoors. It was mid-January, and tufts of yellowish-brown grass peeked through icy patches of sludge.

"Did you have a bad day?"

"No."

"Are you mad at us for taking you to this appointment?"

"Mom, I'm fine. I'm just tired."

"*Hon*," Bill intervened, his hand on my knee, squelching my badgering.

But this was not the son I was used to. I was used to a kid who sat at the kitchen table poring over history books and quoting war heroes. "Listen to this one, Mom: 'The object of war is not to die for your country. It's to make the other poor dumb bastard die for his.' Can you believe Patton said that, Mom?"

Sometimes, when William had blathered on about things, I'd felt like batting him away, like a fly, buzzing around my ears. Now, I longed for my energetic son.

Our appointment with Dr. Michaels was at two thirty in Minneapolis. Usually, I took William to doctor appointments alone. Bill came to appointments when I asked, but he pushed back.

"You know more about this stuff than I do," he'd say. "You have Thursdays and Fridays off. I can't use all my vacation time." Usually, I let him slide. I didn't like watching him squirm when doctors asked him questions. But I needed his support.

That day, I pressed Bill to join us. Dr. Michaels wanted both of our perspectives. Plus, Bill picked up on subtleties that went over my head. He was the first to notice that William's persistent requests for hugs in the evenings coincided with his medication wearing off.

Dr. Michaels's waiting room was busy but not sardine-like. Steel-framed chairs with black leather seat cushions were arranged around glass coffee tables, providing a false sense of privacy. Live plants revealed comforting imperfections. Even the choice of magazines offered inspiration. Instead of the *Homemaker* and *Parenting* magazines in most doctors' offices, the *Star Tribune, Rolling Stone, National Geographic,* and *New Yorker* covered the tables.

Bill staked out a private corner away from strangers. We sat in a row, William in the middle, losing ourselves in different worlds: Bill in the *Star Tribune*, William in *Rolling Stone*, me in the *New Yorker*. Unlike many ADHD kids, William could read for long stretches without being derailed by a whisper. His body became still, as if relieved to have a breather from the constant fidgeting.

Bill masked his nerves well, smiling each time our eyes met. Normally, when we had a free moment, he teased about my love of cardio-kick aerobics classes, punching into the air when others weren't looking. That day, as we waited for Dr. Michaels to emerge, there was a sadness in Bill's eyes.

I understood. Taking our son to see a doctor who made a living prescribing psychiatric medication for out-of-sync children isn't a high point for any parent. I had hoped that William's pediatrician could manage his ADHD symptoms. I had convinced myself that if the pediatrician couldn't treat his ADHD, his prognosis was worse than your average child with ADHD.

I was wrong. On the contrary, if I had scheduled an appointment with a child psychiatrist (or similar professional) from the get-go, we probably would have made greater headway in controlling William's symptoms. These professionals have way more day-to-day experience in their practice to draw from than pediatricians do.

That day at Dr. Michaels's office, I wanted a solution. Bill and I noticed the most dramatic improvement in William's functioning when he was on Adderall. But we needed to find a way to curb the side effects. Dr. Michaels was the most talented psychiatrist I knew in the Twin Cities. He noticed subtle changes in children that others missed, like a slight difference in their gait after switching medications. He and I had worked together on an inpatient unit at a hospital several years back. I knew he wasn't taking new patients, but I decided to call him anyway. How could it hurt? Lucky for us, he agreed to take William on as a patient.

"I'm going to go find something to drink," Bill announced in a low, growly voice, ignoring the giant jug of cold filtered water that sat ready for consumption in the corner. He detested waiting idly for even five minutes. Even at the grocery store, he monitored the checkout lines, clenching his jaw if we got behind someone with a purse full of coupons.

William shifted his focus to the waiting room. "Is he mentally ill, Mom?" he whispered loudly in my ear, not-so-subtly motioning to a man across the room who was talking to himself under his breath. The man was wearing a bright orange Home Depot baseball cap and layers of worn clothing. Every few minutes, he flipped off his cap and ran his nicotine-stained fingers through his greasy hair. A small circle of open seats surrounded him.

"It looks like it, but we can't talk about it here," I responded, lightly shaking my head back and forth.

"What do you think is the matter with him?"

"*William,* I just told you we couldn't talk about it here. Ask me later."

"Am I mentally ill, Mom? Is that why I'm here?"

"No, you're not mentally ill," I answered reflexively, taken aback by his question. In the DSM-5, ADHD is technically classified as a mental disorder of the neuro-developmental type. To me, a mental illness—like major depression, which can go into full remission with the right treatment—feels pretty different from ADHD, a developmental disorder that persists into adulthood in about thirty to fifty percent of cases.

Yet William wasn't asking about semantics. He was asking why he was waiting to see a doctor in the same room as a man who was carrying on a full conversation with himself.

As I mulled William's question over in my mind, I felt ill-prepared to parent him. He and I were so different. I was way more private. When I was a child, I responded to stress by pulling inward. If he was curious about something, he didn't hesitate to ask, regardless of the topic. Sometimes, William brought me so far outside of my comfort zone that I froze and gave a jumbled answer that we both knew was nonsense. I wasn't sure *how* to give the perfect answer (as if there were one), so I put him off, at least for a few days, until I "perfected" it. By that time, he'd already trudged to the library, loaded up with books on the subject, and educated himself.

I spotted Dr. Michaels behind the front desk wearing a dark suit, pastel striped tie, and modern black-rimmed glasses. As he walked toward us, a smile grew on his face.

"You must be William. I'm Dr. Michaels. How do you do?" he asked, extending his large hand. William shook his hand and smiled shyly, looking back down at his magazine.

"So, you're a *Rolling Stone* man, eh?" he asked, sitting down beside William. Given his six-foot-four frame, Dr. Michaels towered over children. His intuitive sense about how to put children at ease was impressive.

"Well, I like music."

"What kind? Country, rap, rock and roll?"

"Mostly rock and roll. My mom likes country, though," William responded, looking up at me, as though he wished I would take over.

"Dr. Quie, I didn't know that about you," Dr. Michaels teased. "Is your mom into *newer* country singers, like Garth Brooks and Carrie Underwood, or *old* country legends, like Merle Haggard and Willie Nelson?"

As William looked to me for a response, Bill and I shared a smile. Years earlier, shortly after we met, he had wooed me by dressing in country attire. His brother videotaped him lip-syncing one of my favorite Garth Brooks songs, "Friends in Low Places."

"Which group is Reba McEntire in? She dragged me to one of her concerts years ago," Bill chimed in.

After a few more minutes of casual conversation, Dr. Michaels asked William if he'd like to get started. Bill and I grabbed our things and followed behind.

"Hop up on the scale for me, William. Let's see what you're made of," Dr. Michaels instructed. William pulled off his snow boots and stepped onto the scale. "You're approaching eighty pounds. Does that sound right?"

"I don't know. I think I weighed eighty-two pounds last time I was at the doctor."

"Well, if you've pooped today, that could explain the difference," Dr. Michaels added, a wry grin on his face.

"Let me see. I think I did poop this morning," William answered, his hand cupping his chin, eyes twinkling.

Bill and I stood behind them in the hallway as a flurry of nurses, doctors, and patients wove past us. I turned to Bill and smiled. I knew they would hit it off.

"All right, we've got your weight. Now let's take your blood pressure," Dr. Michaels said, taking the cuff off the wall, folding up William's sleeve, and wrapping the wide band around his skinny arm. On the hospital unit, I'd noticed that Dr. Michaels took children's vitals himself instead of asking for nursing assistance. I'd assumed it was because they were short-staffed. Now, I realized that taking vitals was part of his rapport-building.

"If I squeeze your arm off, William, make sure

you ask one of your parents to pick it up for you," Dr. Michaels told William. "We don't want you leaving here without it. Since you're right-handed, your left arm isn't quite as essential, but it still comes in handy," he teased, straight-faced, looking William in the eye.

"Ouch, you're cutting off my circulation," William said, eyes watering. "I hate having my blood pressure taken," he added, clenching his fist. He had always been a wimp at doctor's visits. Even taking his temperature was an ordeal. He gagged on the thermometer and pushed it back out of his mouth. Often, doctors gave up and felt his cheeks for warmth.

"Let me see those muscles of yours," Dr. Michaels pressed. "Aren't you a hockey player? I think your mom's mentioned that before," he asked, glancing at me for clarity. I nodded.

"Yeah, I play hockey," William answered, thrusting his shoulders back, standing taller.

"Don't hockey players have to be tough? Don't they have big muscles like this?" Dr. Michaels added, rolling up the sleeves on his starched dress shirt, flexing his arm muscles.

"Yeah, I guess so," William answered with a timid smile.

"Pretend you're Wayne Gretzky, William. Think tough guy thoughts about hockey while I squeeze your arm ever so slightly," Dr. Michaels said as he wrapped the cuff around William's arm a second time. William shuddered and looked in the opposite direction.

"According to the blood pressure gauge, William,

you are as dead as a doornail. What do you make of that? Do you think it was an accurate read?" Dr. Michaels asked with a smile.

Bill and I looked at each other knowingly, accustomed to the circumstances.

"Well, I don't feel like I'm dead. But that would be cool, wouldn't it? Being a ghost, watching what everyone was doing without them knowing it," William said.

"I'm not a fan of being dead, William. It just doesn't sound appealing to me, but I hear your point. The ghost thing would be cool," Dr. Michaels answered, signaling us into his office. His credentials framed above his desk in the corner were the only lasting evidence of him in the room. Like most psychiatrists, Dr. Michaels practiced in a few locations. He sat in a swiveling chair, and Bill, William, and I sat across from him in mustard-yellow vinyl upright chairs. The bright light glared, revealing our imperfections. William looked childlike in his chair, pulling his knees up tightly to his chest and wrapping his arms around them.

It was a whole lot easier problem-solving with Dr. Michaels about somebody else's kid than my own. I was afraid of tearing up, my norm in intakes. Most parents did the same thing at my office.

I didn't realize until later that I'd put Dr. Michaels up on a pedestal. When I asked Dr. Michaels for help, what I was really asking was, Can't you make this ADHD thing go away? We're ready to move on to something less frustrating, like a tic disorder. We can handle repeated shoulder-shrugging or even eye-bulging.

"William, I'm going to ask you some questions about why you've come to see me," Dr. Michaels said, tipping back in his chair, his clipboard tucked against his belt.

"Okay," William nodded, fumbling with his shoelaces.

"Do you know why you're here today?"

"Not really," he answered with a shrug, even though we'd discussed it a handful of times.

"Well, your parents asked if I could help with your medication for ADHD. Your mom also mentioned that you had been feeling sad lately. Do you know what she's talking about?" he asked, glancing at me. I sat quietly in my seat, purse in my lap, rubbing my fingers along the leather strap.

"No, not really," William answered.

I couldn't believe it. Just two nights before, he called for me while he was in the basement practicing guitar. When I arrived, he was sitting in his normal practicing spot, his Stratocaster across his lap, tears welling in his eyes.

"What's wrong, Will?" I had asked, pulling up a chair beside him.

"I don't know," he had said, as he wiped a tear from his cheek.

"Did something happen at school? Are you sick?" I'd asked, feeling his cool forehead.

"Nothing happened. I just feel so sad."

Dr. Michaels asked William if ever he felt sad for no reason.

"I don't think so," William answered, digging his hand in his pocket, pulling out a neon-orange guitar pick. I couldn't tell if William was distracted or clueless. Like other kids with ADHD, he lived in the moment, which was crazy-making at times like this.

Dr. Michaels raised his eyebrows and looked to me for clarification. Then, Bill stepped in. "William has been sad lately. He cries easily and doesn't smile as much as he used to. His mood hasn't been the same since he started Focalin in fifth grade. That was about a year ago."

Dr. Michaels then turned to William. "Do you notice that focusing is harder for you than other kids?" he asked.

"Not really. I mean *sometimes*, but not all the time," William answered.

"You sounded like a politician, William, do you realize that?" he teased.

William brightened. He loved people who thought on their feet. "Have you seen the political cartoons from the *New Yorker*?" William asked, looking directly at Dr. Michaels.

"You're quite the kid, William. But you're not making this interview easy for me," said Dr. Michaels. "Your parents seem to believe that you have ADHD *and* that you've been feeling sad lately. But maybe they're incorrect. What do you think?"

William explained that he did struggle to focus, especially when he was "forced to listen" to his teacher "go on and on." "I'm *literally being tortured to death*, and I can't ever read my book," he added, tearing up.

Each time William explained his predicament, it reminded me to be more patient with him, especially on school days.

"Yeah, I catch your drift, William," said Dr. Michaels. "Being trapped in your desk and bored to death is no fun. But isn't having to sit still and listen to things, even when we aren't interested, part of life? I'd get fired if I walked out of meetings any time I felt bored. It wouldn't be cool if I whipped out my Kindle and started reading in the middle of a session with a patient, would it?"

William paused. Dr. Michaels had made a good point, and he knew it. "I guess not. But it feels so uncomfortable. I can't stand it when I have to just sit there. I already know half the stuff she's teaching about. It just makes me angry," William added, pulling his knees to his chest.

"Do you think it's normal for people to feel that irritable when they're asked to sit still and listen to something they find boring? Do your other friends get irritated too?"

William reached in his other pocket, now thumbing a guitar pick in each hand. "Not really," he conceded, burying his face in his knees.

"So what do you think? Do you think people with ADHD are unique in that they get bored more easily than others? Do you think they have a harder time sitting still and focusing than the rest of us?"

"I guess so," William answered, staring at the floor as if he'd lost ten straight rounds of Uno to Emma.

"Do you think there's anything wrong with having ADHD?"

"Well, I don't like having it," he said, peering at Dr. Michaels over his knees.

"Because . . . ?"

"Because I don't like being different. I don't want to stand out."

Bill and I glanced at each other in awe at Dr. Michaels's ability to challenge William and help him see another perspective.

"Being different isn't so bad, William," said Dr. Michaels. "I have less hair than you do, but I'm learning to deal with it," he added with a smile.

"Having less hair isn't as bad as having ADHD," William shot back, his eyes traveling to the top of Dr. Michaels's head. "You could just get some hair replacement therapy or wear a toupee," William said with a smile.

We all laughed, relieved William had weathered the meeting and made a new ally. Dr. Michaels's commitment to helping William understand his diagnosis took a huge weight off of my shoulders.

That afternoon, before we left, Dr. Michaels prescribed William a low dosage of Wellbutrin, an antidepressant which is also an off-label medication used to treat ADHD. Like stimulants, it impacts the neurotransmitters norepinephrine and dopamine, but it affects them differently. Dr. Michaels forewarned us that it might not help; it could even worsen William's mood.

We would have to wait and see.

My Heart Hurts

After an uncustomary silence during music practice, I meandered downstairs to take a peek.

"Everything okay down here?" I asked, aware of my invasion into William's sacred musical territory. His wiry, newly muscular body, half boy and half man, caught me off guard. At thirteen, he was nearly my height, something I hadn't envisioned happening so soon.

"I just want to be alone, Mom," he answered with a glance.

"Any reason why?" I asked, peering down at him, my hair swinging in my face.

"I just do. Don't I have the right to be alone sometimes?"

"Sure. I'm here if you want to talk," I added, lingering, straightening a pile of shoes by the back door. Despite my desire to dig deeper, I knew better. We didn't have to talk through everything. William had a right to his privacy and to be a grump sometimes. I knew that teenagers were notorious for volatility, but it hadn't surfaced yet in William. Maybe it was his ADHD. For years, when he was upset, he'd literally clung to us, asking for squeezes.

Now, I dreaded what I saw at work: prickly teens

who couldn't stand to be in the same room with their middle-aged parents. Before appointments, when I cracked the door open into the waiting room and searched for their youthful faces, sullen teens left their parents without acknowledgment.

During sessions, talk of an impending family vacation brought on disgusted facial expressions, as if the teenagers had caught a whiff of a dead animal. I listened, mostly without judgment, remembering the days when I had walked ten paces behind my own mother, embarrassed by her bohemian flowered skirts, Jesus sandals, and bright coral lipstick, the very things I'd adorned myself in a few years earlier during dress-up. Later, as a teen, I had been curt and mean in a desperate, subconscious effort to break away. Why should I be spared such treatment from my own teenager?

Upstairs in the kitchen, I tried to distract myself by unloading dishes and wiping down counters. Normally, when it was time for William to hone his guitar skills, he trudged slowly down the basement stairs. Getting started had never been easy. Familiar sounds of preparation followed: papers fluttered, his guitar stand creaked and clanked against other equipment, pentatonic scales whipped up and down his guitar strings. Sometimes, his microphone crashed to the ground, followed by grunts of frustration. Then came songs like "Foxy Lady" by Jimi Hendrix, "I'll Play the Blues for You" by Albert King, and "Layla" by Eric Clapton. Even if I'd had a lousy day at the office, my toes tapped and my waist swiveled.

"You go, girl," Bill teased from the other room as he watched me out of the corner of his eye, pleased to see the weight of my day lift. Many nights, Emma, Bill, and I crowded together on the narrow basement stairs and sang along until William shooed us away.

That evening, William trudged through his chords, scales, and songs. He didn't sing. Minutes later, I heard the click of his amp turning off, and he tromped upstairs to his room, the door shutting behind him.

Bill spotted me attempting to read in the living room and sat down beside me on the couch.

"Do you know what's going on?" I asked, chewing at my cuticles.

"I talked to him earlier this afternoon when he got home from school. He's feeling down. He just doesn't know if he wants to become a musician after all," he said, scanning my face for a reaction.

"Why's he worrying about that? He's only thirteen. He's just a kid," I said, relieved it wasn't something worse.

"Who knows? Don't teenagers get moody? You'd know better than me," he answered, propping his feet on the coffee table and rolling up his sleeve so I could rub the underside of his forearm.

"Just because I'm a psychologist doesn't mean I understand everything about teens," I answered, tucking an oversized pillow beneath my head and resting my feet in Bill's lap. "I hope he doesn't feel pressured by us to become a musician. That's a hard life. I just want him to be happy."

Deep down, I knew that I pushed him too hard sometimes. I'd raised my voice when he'd put off practicing. I could hear the disappointment in my voice when he turned down opportunities to play music around the Twin Cities.

Part of this was driven by fear. Music had given him confidence in a way that school hadn't. Part was my own selfishness. His music brought us happiness, sometimes at his expense. More than once, he'd told Bill and me to back off. It was his life.

At bedtime, I tapped on William's door. When I got no answer, I cracked the door open. He lay sprawled, face-down on his twin bed. "What's wrong?" I asked, sitting beside him on the bed, resting my hand on his lower back.

"I don't know," he mumbled into his comforter, hands by his sides.

"Really? Don't you have any idea what's bothering you?" I asked. "Is it about music?"

"I'm just lazy, Mom," he said, his words confusing me further. Despite William's school troubles, he'd been a confident kid.

"Where is this coming from?"

"I never want to do anything, at least not anything that matters. I'm worried I'll end up a failure," he added, his voice still muffled into his comforter.

"In what way? You have so much going for you. Are you worried about middle school?"

"I'm worried about my twenties," he answered, still speaking out of the side of his mouth.

The word "twenties" helped me start to put the pieces together. Earlier that week, we had gone to see Dr. Michaels. William was about to start seventh grade at Great River, a Montessori school. At the appointment, he and Dr. Michaels spoke while I sat to the side, mostly listening.

"Your parents are in charge of your health now, William. But by the time you're in your twenties, you'll be in charge. You'll determine if medication is necessary, not them," Dr. Michaels said, rolling up his sleeves, sitting back in his swivel chair.

During their conversation, William had nodded along, seemingly unfazed, rubbing a guitar pick between his thumb and fingers, a source of comfort.

"You have two pretty good options," Dr. Michaels continued, searching his desk for a clean sheet of paper. "You can start middle school off meds and see how things go, or you can start school on meds, which may take the edge off when you're learning new routines." As Dr. Michaels spoke, he wrote the words pros and cons at the top of the page. "My main concern with adolescents with your condition is underachievement," he said, writing *underachievement* on the cons side. "You're a smart guy, don't you think?" he'd asked with a grin, scanning William's face, pen in hand.

"Maybe," William answered shyly, shrugging his

shoulders, lightly turning his guitar pick in circles on the desk with his pointer finger.

"You are," Dr. Michaels said with a smile, leaning back in his chair, pride spreading across his face. "You read a lot, play guitar, and have friends and supportive parents. You have what we call protective factors," he said, listing music, friends, and parents on the pros side. "I'm willing to support you if you want to start school without medication. But if you can't focus, if you start thinking things like, 'That's a nice ceiling fan up there, I wonder who manufactured it,' instead of listening to the lecture, you can't view going back on your meds as a failure," he said, setting his pen down, leaning up against the desk, looking William directly in the eyes.

"Okay," William answered, shaking on it when Dr. Michaels extended his hand.

"So what do you want to do, William?" Dr. Michaels asked.

"I want to start school without meds," William answered firmly, shoulders back, glancing at me and crossing his arms. I raised my eyebrows and shrugged, turning the decision back to him. I viewed it as a new chapter for both of us. Dr. Michaels was right. Sooner or later, Bill and I would have to step back and let William make his own decisions.

That evening, as William lay in bed, he turned to face me and brought his hands to his chest as if he were protecting a wound. "Mom, I don't know what's wrong, but my heart hurts," he said, a tear running down his cheek. "I just didn't realize my condition was so serious, that it wasn't going to go away. I just don't think I can reach my goals without you and Dad," he said, wiping his eyes.

"What makes you think having ADHD is so serious?" I asked, dabbing his tears with my sleeve. I was tempted to list off people who'd thrived in the midst of ADHD, but I resisted. If I moved into rescue mode, I'd stifle his grief. He had a right to his feelings.

"The way Dr. Michaels talked about it today, like I have a *condition* that I'll always have to deal with. I don't *want* to have to take medication the rest of my life," he'd said, cupping my hand in his, bringing it to his chest.

"I heard him say *condition*, too, but it's just a way of describing a diagnosis."

"Mom, it's not just the word *condition* that upset me. You don't get it," he said, yanking his hand from mine. "I hate having ADHD, and it's *never* going away. I hate the medicine. I hate going to doctor's appointments. It's all bullshit," he said, turning his back to me, facing the wall.

I didn't know what to say. In hindsight, I should have kept my mouth shut and listened. But that was a real challenge for me when my anxiety skyrocketed. So I tried another tactic.

"I hate it too," I said, seeking a laugh. Humor had usually worked with my parents when they escalated.

"That's real reassuring, Mom," William said, looking at me like he wanted to slug me.

"William, I can't possibly understand how you feel, but you're not alone. A lot of people have ADHD. Dad and I will continue to help you."

"You can't always help me, Mom. Like Dr. Michaels said, I have to start figuring this stuff out on my own."

I should have known that William would take Dr. Michaels's comments at face value. That's what teenagers do. So I did my best to put things in perspective. He was nowhere near college age. I told him his ADHD would change as he matured. He might not even need medication then.

"Who says?" he asked, turning onto his back.

"Dr. Michaels. Me. I have patients with ADHD who go off their meds in college. You'll still have ADHD, but you'll learn how to manage it."

Some of this was true. The frontal lobe of the brain—the part that helps us focus, think ahead, plan, and organize—continues to develop well beyond our teenage years. Like Dr. Michaels had said, William had a lot going for him.

I also knew that many people with ADHD floundered into adulthood. High school graduation rates were lower for students with ADHD. College graduation was even lower. I danced back and forth between both realities: the bleak one based on research and the optimistic one based on hope. I had no way of knowing what William's future held. How could I? But I saw William's potential. I believed in him. So did Dr. Michaels. One of the toughest things I had to do at junctures like this was step back and hope that eventually, William would learn to believe in himself.

PART FIVE:
High School

I Play Blues

It was Parent Information Night at Saint Paul Conservatory for Performing Artists (SPCPA), a charter high school that offered intensive arts instruction in voice, dance, musical theater, jazz, and classical music. Juniors and seniors took their places on stage to answer questions for prospective freshman and parents. Teachers in fitted blazers, skinny ties, angled dresses, and oversized glasses took turns addressing the crowd. The students reminded me of William with their dyed hair, skinny jeans, and vintage T-shirts.

"What's the matter?" I whispered to William as I draped my black leather coat over my seat. He hadn't said a word since we left the house.

"I'm a blues player, not jazz," William answered, looking straight ahead. "I don't even like jazz." He frowned, folding the program in half.

"How do you know?" I asked, playing dumb. Just the

other night, I'd overheard him compare jazz to elevator music. I barely knew anything about jazz, but I thought William would be happier at a smaller high school that concentrated on the arts than the huge public schools in our district. The only other high school with similar credentials, Perpich Center for Arts Education, was miles away in Golden Valley. William's middle school music teacher and about every other musician we knew recommended we visit SPCPA.

During the next hour, teachers and students pitched the school. They offered regular, Advanced Placement, and Post-Secondary Educational Opportunity classes. The school day was longer than most high schools, given the three hours of daily arts instruction. They wanted disciplined students committed to their craft.

As I listened, William sulked.

"Why don't you ask about blues instruction?" I wrote on my program.

He shook his head no.

"Then I will," I wrote, pressing my note into his lap.

My heartbeat quickened as I prepared my simple question. Then I raised my hand. I didn't want to speak for William, but I wasn't going to let him silence me. I liked the feel of SPCPA. The jazz instructor's ruffled hair and offset tie let me know he didn't expect perfection from his students. His classical piano background and emphasis on note-reading and improvisation would be good for William. Plus, class sizes were small. There were only one hundred students in each grade level.

When the jazz teacher pointed to me, William's hand shot up. I smiled, looked to William, and sat back in my seat.

"Do you guys teach blues here?"

"Good question," he answered with a smile. "The simplified answer to your question is that yes, we do teach blues here, just not directly," he said, straightening his tie. "Jazz and blues are in the same family. I guess you could describe jazz as blues played with a swing rhythm."

William nodded along.

After the presentation, we filed down the aisle alongside other teens and parents. Many huddled around the teachers with questions. William walked right past them.

"So what'd you think?" I asked, dodging patches of ice along the sidewalk as I tried to catch up with him. I wrapped my fuzzy scarf around my neck and hooked my arm in William's. The midwinter cold penetrated my bones. "Cool that blues and jazz are so alike," I said, peering into William's serious blue eyes, searching for a clue as to his impression.

"I guess."

"What do you mean, 'I guess'?" I asked, turning the car light on so I could see his expression. "You *love* music. You play *all the time*. What's the matter?"

William stared into his lap, flicking his guitar pick back and forth against his thumb.

"What is it?"

"I can't read music, Mom," he answered, barely above a whisper.

"Then what are you doing when I see you looking at a score of music, like at Blues Camp in Chicago every summer?"

"Not much," he answered, shaking his head. "I try to read it, but it doesn't click. I play by ear. That's how I've always played," he said, glancing up at me.

William's words filled in gaps of confusion I'd pushed up against during the meeting at SPCPA. My brain pinged from one idea to the next at its usual tempo. We could set up extra music lessons with his guitar instructor to focus on note-reading. I could email the jazz teacher to get more information about the note-reading portion of the audition. I even considered trying to teach William myself, but he had already explained that note-reading for piano was different than note-reading for guitar.

"We'll figure something out," I said, breaking the silence, reaching for William's knee. "Besides, you're good at improvising."

"How can I improvise on the music for the audition if I don't know any jazz?"

"Didn't you listen to anything the jazz guy said?"

Will looked up at me with a grin, the first of the evening.

"Blues and jazz are in the same family. And you're a kick-ass blues player."

✳

William had a month to prepare for the instrumental jazz audition at SPCPA. During lessons, he and his guitar instructor practiced note-reading and two contrasting jazz standards from *The Real Book*, a compilation of well-known jazz pieces. When William reminded me that there was no use because he "sucked" at note-reading, I reminded him that he played by ear better than most and that nobody had it all.

Bill drove William to the audition. It was a typical scene: Bill telling William that they needed to go, *now*, William rummaging through his practice space in the basement, searching for the right cord for his electric guitar. Bill had hauled William and his guitar so many places by then.

For a few minutes after they left, I mulled over the audition. I reminded myself that no matter what, we would make it work. If he didn't get into SPCPA and had to go to a larger school, we'd find a way.

I think William's background in the blues, passion for music, and aural skills—the ability to play by ear— were what earned him a spot in the jazz track at SPCPA. It certainly wasn't his sight-reading. After the audition, William knew he'd blown that part.

Each year at SPCPA, William took required courses in music theory, composition, and aural training, played in an ensemble, *and* had a full academic course load. This wouldn't work for some students, but for teens like William, who need major mental and physical stimulation, SPCPA was a good fit. Plus, the classes were smaller than those of traditional public high schools in our district, and the teachers had a particular interest in working with artistic, quirky kids. They followed his 504 Accommodation Plan too.

The summer before ninth grade, William had private cognitive testing to help pave the way for a successful high school experience. I make this recommendation for nearly all teenagers with ADHD. Here's why:

High school is rigorous, especially for students with learning differences. Testing helps the student, his teachers, and his parents understand how to help him most. In William's case, test results were pretty consistent with his Children's Hospital testing, which wasn't surprising. Our brains tend to follow a consistent trajectory.

William maintained strong language skills and weaker executive functioning skills. Although most students with ADHD have more "discrepancies" in learning than your average person, his split was bigger than most; he was in the 99th percentile in vocabulary but the 14th percentile in visual processing speed.

After reviewing the results, William's 504 Accommodation Coordinator in high school strongly recommended added time for test-taking. People with a weakness in visual processing speed, like William, have difficulty tracking and copying visual information quickly. In real life, this translates to needing more time to do things like marking bubbles on the answer sheet.

Since William had a medical diagnosis of ADHD

and requested added time consistently throughout high school, he qualified for added time on the American College Testing (ACT) college entrance exam. This meant that instead of having four hours for the exam, he got six.

Did this accommodation help him earn an invitation to the National Honors Society in high school? *Most likely.*

Did it help him thrive in AP classes? *I think so.*

Here's why: AP tests are long and grueling, and students with ADHD have a lot to manage. Little kids with ADHD seem to describe this best. At work, when I ask about school troubles, this is what they say:

"I just can't stand the way pencils sound on paper. It makes me feel sick."

"I want to do my work, but my brain keeps looking around the room. Then, when I get started, everybody's done with their work."

"I can't stop moving, so my page is blurry when I try to read the words."

"Everybody's working faster than me. I get so worried that I can't think."

I'd grown so accustomed to hearing William's music that when he went to Montana to climb the Rocky Mountains the summer before his junior year in high school, the house felt empty.

"It's too quiet. When is William coming home?" Emma had commented on William's absence more than once.

Whenever William returned from sleepovers, school, anywhere, music followed within minutes: Ray Charles's "Georgia on My Mind" on my antique upright piano in the dining room, a hip-hop beat on his drum set in the basement, a blues riff on his lavender Stratocaster.

When he returned from camp, he held his guitar like a long-lost friend. They disappeared into his room for hours.

Emma was perched on a stool at the island in the kitchen, immersed in eighth-grade homework. Ah, I love this family, I thought. One benefit of my work was that I didn't take little things for granted. When either of my children typed a paper for school, practiced their music, or offered to help me out, I felt lucky.

I heard a tap on the window and spotted Bill on the patio. He held up a glass of wine and motioned me to join.

"I'll be right there," I mouthed through the window, excited to put my feet up. I poured myself a glass of pinot noir and headed out to the backyard, dogs at my feet.

"Mom, can you come up here?" I heard from the upstairs right when I sat down by Bill.

"No, she can't. Mom's with me. We have a date, bud," Bill answered, staring upward toward the voice.

"Mom, I *need* you to hear this," William yelled from my study.

Bill and I looked at each other. We wanted to have time together, but we both remembered the days when we had to sit with him during guitar practice. Now he was in a band, writing music, practicing on his own. Wine could wait.

I flipped off my sandals by the back door and followed the music up to my office. When I saw my Do Not Disturb sign on the door, I grinned. I'd hoped it would make me write more.

William sat shirtless in cutoff shorts at my old pine table. It was the only piece of furniture I'd asked for when my dad had downsized the first time. He'd eaten grits and soft-boiled eggs at this table for forty-plus years. I'd planned to use it as a writing desk, but mostly, I ran my hands over the top and felt the soft imperfections in the wood from years of use. Now that Dad was gone, I felt comforted knowing his hands had touched the same imperfections.

William and the desk had a different relationship. He scribbled song lyrics on the back of my paperwork, then strummed his guitar and sang. Back and forth he went. When he felt satisfied, he recorded himself on his iPad. That's when he must have called me. For whatever reason, I was his guinea pig. He wanted encouragement, but not too much. If I praised him, he got flustered and said, "Don't be fake, Mom."

I sat down on my chaise lounge in the corner of the room and leaned back, tucking a pillow behind my head.

"It's not great, but I want you to hear something I'm working on," he said.

"Sure. Is it blues? Jazz?"

William was one of the only people I knew, outside

of the kids I saw at work, who answered fewer than half of my questions. "Did you turn in your paper?" and "What time is your show?" were rarely answered on the first or even second try. From what I understood about ADHD, he likely heard me the second time but was too caught up in his own thoughts to respond.

William explained that the song he'd written was inspired by a young Chicago band called Twin Peaks. He loved their casual style and passion. They were low-key rockers. He'd started writing the song that afternoon in study hall. It had been a hard day. I knew why, but chose not to ask questions. He wasn't in the mood.

William sang about a young man and a girl he'd grown to love; the man kissed her on the head and said goodbye. Neither understood why. It just had to end. "You had to watch me walk away," he sang, staring down at his hands, strumming his acoustic guitar.

Compassion, pride, and happiness swirled in my heart as I listened. I felt sad for my son, who'd broken up with his girlfriend, but proud of his courage to share his truth. I envied William's creative edge. Music gave him a way to make sense of his life that evaded so many.

"Do you like it?" he asked.

"I love it," I said. And then he hurried off to the basement.

I wondered what my life would have been like if I hadn't had a kid like him who'd pushed me to my limit. Would I have discovered creative writing? Written a book? Taken up yoga? I doubted it. I'd never been drawn to creative writing *before* parenthood. I'd decided to write a book about ADHD because I felt so alone. My closest friends were far away, and the ones I had nearby didn't have kids with learning differences.

I'd taken up yoga when William started high school, shortly after my mom was diagnosed with stage-four cancer. When my older sister called to share the news, I literally walked to a private room away from my family and dropped to my knees. Before that moment, I hadn't understood the expression "to drop to one's knees in grief."

For the next few years, I worried constantly about Mom, who lived miles away in Baltimore. I wanted to be with her twenty-four seven, not at home helping Bill and the kids manage high school, work, music practice, and sports. When my appetite dropped and my heart started pounding out of nowhere, I recognized the symptoms. Post-partum had taught me well. Then I did what any half-brained psychologist should do when she's on a slippery slope toward a mental breakdown: I called my psychiatrist, who adjusted my medication. Then, I made an appointment with a grief counselor, who was wonderful.

A few weeks later, once my body settled, I took a serious look at my life. I realized that I had spent so much time trying to calm everyone around me that I didn't really know how to calm myself, at least not in a crisis. Since my grief was so physical, I tried breathing exercises and guided imagery, but these only provided temporary relief. Weekly aerobics with my Y-ladies wasn't the answer, either.

My college friend Cara describes these aerobics classes as "totally manic." She's right, but there's nothing wrong with socializing and sweating. Both are good for your heart.

Then one day, I walked past a new yoga studio in our neighborhood. I'd always viewed yoga as a waste of time. I didn't have time to sit around and stretch. But the salt-rock lamps and purple geodes in the window caught my attention. So I walked up to the front desk and asked about classes. Then I bought a week's worth.

The dreadlocked, twenty-something woman at the front desk smiled and offered me a cup of tea. Others like her milled about barefoot in tank tops and wide-legged, comfortable pants. The energy was calm, the lighting dim. I needed something like this in my life.

I fell in love with yoga that week, even though I smacked my forehead and bent the shit out of my wrists attempting crow pose. I loved the new-agey music and having lavender essential oil massaged on my forehead. I loved being praised for making it to my mat. I loved feeling my way through positions with my eyes closed at 6:00 a.m. classes and trying to hold positions so intensely that I forgot about my mother, the kids' high school responsibilities, and how I barely paid attention to Bill.

I learned to breathe—into my front body, my back, and my side body, and along my spine too.

And one of the greatest things about my new yoga life was that Emma became a yogi too.

✳

Pushing Through

By William's senior year, he could whip out an AP English paper in a few hours, thanks to Ms. Margaret and his excellent high school English teachers.

He'd also developed a solid paper-writing routine that went something like this:

—Make a huge mess in the kitchen while savoring olive tapenade, strong-smelling cheese, prosciutto, and water crackers

—Take meds

—Sequester himself in the study (barking at intruders to Please Get Out)

—Put on noise-canceling headphones

—Type

William and Dr. Michaels learned that a low dosage of medication after school helped him sustain attention for tough homework assignments. To me as a parent, William's paper-writing routine was a beautiful thing to witness; not that most parents wouldn't feel good seeing their highschooler thrive. But one of the gifts of having a kid with ADHD (or any disability) is seeing them finally push through their challenges and thrive. Like most high school seniors, he still had mini breakdowns and slip-ups (like gaming for huge chunks of time instead of doing his work), but it was different than it had been earlier in his education, when he *couldn't* work independently, even when he wanted to.

✳

The Final Stretch

Since William managed his own homework his senior year, much of our attention as parents went toward helping him prepare for college.

Until we decided that we couldn't. We simply didn't have the energy. I was still traveling often to visit Mom, which left Bill to pick up the slack at home. Plus, neither Bill nor I were good at organizing massive amounts of paperwork and deadlines, which are a big part of the college application process.

I took my close friend Jana's advice and hired a coach, Anne, who helped students and parents prepare for the college admissions process. It cost us a few thousand dollars, but it was *well worth it.*

William applied to four-year colleges that offered strong liberal arts educations and conservatory music programs. He handled advanced coursework in high school, loved learning about history and religion, and toyed with the idea of becoming a professional musician.

For one, Anne helped William improve his writing score on the ACT *significantly.* She knew the formula for the writing portion of the ACT, and she helped him learn to draft essays accordingly. Then, when William declared that his college essays were finished, Anne took one for the team and gave him the news: you have a shit ton more work to do on these, my dear. When he argued, she argued back. Finally, Anne kept a detailed timeline of when his college applications were due and reminded us all (mostly William) of what needed to be done.

Life was hectic the fall of William's senior year. It seemed like we were always driving William to appointments with Anne (nope, he wasn't driving yet), visiting colleges, recording his first auditions, and then driving or flying him to second auditions when he made the cut.

He hadn't pushed driving much earlier in high school, and I knew the research. A 2007 study by Russell Barkley and Daniel J. Cox concluded that young drivers with ADHD were two to four times as likely as those without ADHD to have an accident—meaning that they were at a higher risk of wrecking the car than an adult who was legally drunk. Scary, right?

That's why Bill and I made a pact not to facilitate driving for William. If he was motivated enough to find a class, then fine, we would consider paying for it. But he had to do the legwork.

It sounded easy enough.

Until mother-guilt clouded my rational brain.

Driver's education wasn't even offered at William's high school. He couldn't sign up for classes at other high schools given his extended day at a performing arts high school. Plus, William felt Bill was being an asshole. What father wouldn't help his son find a driver's education class? Especially when they're the oldest of their friend group. Not being able to drive was humiliating. We were the ones who'd made him repeat kindergarten in the first place. This driving delay was all our fault. The least we could do was help him find a flippin' class.

I broke my pact with Bill when I signed William up for driver's education during William's junior year. Then, at the last minute, life got too busy and William asked me to withdraw him from the class.

When William turned eighteen, he no longer needed to take driver's education. All he had to do was pass the written test, practice driving with an adult for six months, and take a road test. Except the flimsy-paged driver's manual was so technical that William's eyes darted everywhere but to the page, just like they had with *The Enormous Potato* during his youth.

Then, a few months later, William rounded the corner at the Department of Motor Vehicles with a smile on his face. This time, he'd passed the written test. After he practiced driving with an adult for six months, he could take the road test. Easy enough.

Except William didn't want to take his medication. William complained that his medication made him feel withdrawn. He wanted to enjoy driving. So I pushed the research about ADHD-teens and driving out of my mind. I mean, who wants to continuously hold up a sign in their teen's face that reads, "Don't Forget: You Have ADHD?" At the time, I told myself that maybe I was being too pushy, too insensitive to William's needs, rigid even. Maybe William's frontal lobe had matured.

A few weeks later, after my unrealistic hopefulness nearly murdered the whole family at multiple intersections around the Twin Cities, Bill and I took a new approach with William, which went something like this:

Dude, we need you to take your medication *every time* you drive, even if it makes you lose your appetite or feel withdrawn for a few hours. Risking your life or anyone else's isn't something we can condone.

And guess what happened? Stop signs, crosswalks, brake pedals—all kinds of things made themselves known to William.

William felt better too. He didn't really enjoy Bill's death-cries, Emma's declaration that she would no longer drive with him under any circumstances, or my lame excuses for his terrible driving.

Emma, by then a freshman in high school, survived the stress the best any sibling could. I apologized for neglecting her and reminded her that she would have the same support later. She understood.

*

William's rejection from Tulane University, my alma mater, came as a surprise. His GPA and ACT scores were in line with their expectations. In his essay, he'd played up his positive experiences in New Orleans at Jazz Festival and my love of the college. He'd felt good about his audition tapes too.

This rejection lowered his hopes of getting into a competitive conservatory, like Oberlin in Ohio, which had a slim acceptance rate. William didn't feel good about his second audition at Oberlin, either. He felt out of sync with the more classically trained students. He'd only packed jeans, a vintage shirt, and tennis shoes (even after I scolded him for wearing a T-shirt that read, "Hi Mom, I'm in Jail" across the front the first time we visited campus). Most of the other students wore white button-downs, ties, and loafers.

A jazz professor had commented on William's blues-infused playing after the audition and asked him why he had applied for the jazz conservatory. William explained that he knew how to play the blues but felt shaky about jazz. He hoped that a solid education in jazz could take his music skills to a new level. Then they parted ways.

A few days later, I was testing a client when William called me from school. He never called to share good news from school. His calls were always related to one of the following problems: a lost bus pass, a forgotten paper, a lost house key, a lost wallet, a forgotten guitar or guitar cord, or a forgotten lunch.

I asked my client to hang on and explained that my eighteen-year-old son was in a pinch of some sort; I'd be right back.

"Hi, William, what's up? I'm at work, you know."

"Mom, I got in! I got into Oberlin! The conservatory and the college!"

✳

That phone call goes to show that we *all* need to keep an open mind and an open heart with the ADHDers in our lives, or we'll chip away at their souls and ours. Some days this may seem impossible, like when they proudly address all of their high school graduation thank-you notes on the wrong side of the envelope.